Perspectives for Change in
Communist Societies

Other Titles in This Series

Westview Special Studies on the Soviet Union and Eastern Europe

Perspectives for Change in Communist Societies
edited by Teresa Rakowska-Harmstone

To what degree has political, social, and economic change been stimulated by the impact of the past and present policies of Communist political systems? Perhaps more important, to what extent has the momentum for change, stimulated by past policies, been frustrated by the nature of these systems? This volume, an interdisciplinary and international work based on a symposium presented at the October 1976 Annual Conference of the American Association for the Advancement of Slavic Studies, addresses these questions. The contributors collectively assess the extent of change generated by the policies of social mobilization as they are channeled and contained within the Communist political systems. Clearly and perceptively, they analyze selected aspects of change—or its absence—in the political, social, and economic life of the Soviet Union and Eastern Europe.

Teresa Rakowska-Harmstone, professor of political science at Carleton University, Ottawa, holds a Ph.D. from Harvard University. Previously director of Carleton University's Institute of Soviet and East European Studies, and a research fellow at George Washington University's Institute for Sino-Soviet Studies and the Institute of International Politics and Economics in Belgrade, she is the author of *Russia and Nationalism in Central Asia* and coeditor, with Adam Bromke, of *The Communist States in Disarray*.

Perspectives for Change in Communist Societies

edited by
Teresa Rakowska-Harmstone

Westview Press / Boulder, Colorado

*Westview Special Studies on the Soviet Union
and Eastern Europe*

Copyright © 1979 by Westview Press, Inc.

Published in 1979 in the United States of America by
  Westview Press, Inc.
  5500 Central Avenue
  Boulder, Colorado 80301
  Frederick A. Praeger, Publisher

Library of Congress Cataloging in Publication Data
Main entry under title:
Perspectives for change in Communist societies.
  (Westview special studies on the Soviet Union and Eastern Europe)
    1. Communism—Addresses, essays, lectures. 2. Communist parties—Addresses,
essays, lectures. 3. Communism—Europe, Eastern—Addresses, essays, lectures.
I. Rakowska-Harmstone, Teresa. II. Series.
HX56.P39   309.1'171'7   78-17331
ISBN 0-89158-336-X

Printed and bound in the United States of America

Contents

Preface

This volume was initiated by a symposium held at the October 1976 annual meeting of the American Association for the Advancement of Slavic Studies at St. Louis, Missouri. Four of the chapters here—by Carl Linden, Sidney Ploss, John Hardt, and Arpad Abonyi and Ivan Sylvain—are the revised original contributions to my panel "Systemic Change in Communist Systems." The idea was to assess systemic limits to change in three areas: political, ideological, and economic, inclusive of a case study. In time the idea has grown, and the book now includes my introductory chapter as well, and three more case studies: of change and stability in Yugoslavia by Gary Bertsch, of crisis management in Poland by Jan Gross, and my analysis of the impact of ethnic nationalisms on change in the Soviet Union. I am indebted to the American Academy of Political and Social Science for the permission to reprint the latter from *The Annals*, September 1977.

I hope that this work may contribute to a better understanding of the process of evolution—or lack thereof—in Communist political systems, and that it may provide insights into the broad, complex question of the relationship between social change and political system, particularly the constraints imposed by Communist systems on social change and the ways in which social forces have attempted to overcome the constraints. The scope here includes the Soviet Union and

Eastern Europe, but some of the findings may have a broader validity.

My warm thanks go to the five original contributors who made the panel a success and who have tolerated, with good grace and good humor, the delays and need for revisions required to transform a panel presentation into a research paper. Equally warm thanks go to Gary Bertsch and Jan Gross for prompt response to my request for contributions on short notice. I am also grateful to Frederick Praeger of Westview Press at whose suggestion the panel became a book, and to the editorial staff for patience and editorial assistance. Special thanks are due to the staff of Carleton University's Political Science Department, especially to Mrs. Pearl Fisher, for valiantly coping with unreasonable typing demands.

Teresa Rakowska-Harmstone

About the Editor and Contributors

Teresa Rakowska-Harmstone, professor of political science at Carleton University, Ottawa, is the author of *Russia and Nationalism in Central Asia: The Case of Tadzhikistan*, co-editor and coauthor of *The Communist States in Disarray* and the forthcoming *Communism in Eastern Europe*, and is a contributor to professional journals and monographs. She has taught at Douglass College, Rutgers University, and was visiting professor at McGill and George Washington University. She was director of Carleton University's Institute of Soviet and East European Studies and a research fellow at George Washington University's Institute for Sino-Soviet Studies and the Institute of International Politics and Economics in Belgrade.

Arpad Abonyi and *Ivan Sylvain* are doctoral candidates in political science at Carleton University, authors of "CMEA Integration and Policy Options for Eastern Europe; A Development Strategy of Dependent States" (*Journal of Common Market Studies*, December 1977), and contributors to a forthcoming volume on East European integration edited by J. M. Montias and Paul Marer.

Gary K. Bertsch is associate professor of political science at the University of Georgia and a former International Research and Exchanges Board exchange scholar in Yugoslavia (1969-70). He is the author of *Nation-Building in Yugoslavia, Value Change and Political Community, Values and Community in Multi-National Yugoslavia,* coeditor of *Comparative Communism: The Soviet, Chinese and Yugoslav Models,* and a contributor to numerous journals and books.

Jan T. Gross is assistant professor of sociology at Yale University. Educated at Warsaw University, Oxford, and Yale, he is the author of the forthcoming *Polish Society under German Occupation—General Government, 1939-1944,* and a contributor to professional journals.

John P. Hardt is senior specialist in Soviet economics, Congressional Research Service, and the author of "Soviet Economic Development and Doctrinal Alternatives," in V. Treml, ed., *The Development of the Soviet Economy: Plan and Performance.* He is the editor of *Mathematics and Computers in Soviet Planning,* as well as numerous other works.

Carl A. Linden, associate professor of International Affairs at the Institute for Sino-Soviet Studies, George Washington University, is the author of *Khrushchev and the Soviet Leadership* and a contributor to many professional journals.

Sidney I. Ploss is with the U.S. Department of State. He is the author of *Conflict and Decision-Making in Soviet Russia,* the editor of *The Soviet Political Process: Aims, Techniques, and Examples of Analysis,* and a contributor to professional journals and monographs.

1
Aspects of Political Change

Teresa Rakowska-Harmstone

The political system established by the Bolsheviks after they seized power in Russia in November 1917 was explicitly dedicated to change. Their party's basic aim (its goal culture, in Chalmers Johnson's definition[1])—the transformation of the semifeudal, semicapitalist imperial Russia into an industrialized socialist society—could be carried out only by radical social and economic policies, the implementation of which required the destruction of traditional social structures and a total social mobilization and politicization of society. Key features of the new system reflected these requirements.

The system's core, then as now, was the "leading role of the party": the monopoly of power appropriated by the Communist party of the strength of its ideologically legitimated role as the vanguard of the working class and exercised on the operational principle of democratic centralism. Paradoxically, a system designed to change society saw no need for its own adaptation and provided no mechanism for its own change, notwithstanding the Marxist assumption that, as a part of the superstructure, a political system is determined by its economic base and reflects its changes. There is no mechanism for conflict resolution either, because class conflict, the only type of conflict recognized, was to be suppressed pending the destruction of the bourgeoisie and was expected to disappear once socialism was built. Moreover, any recognition of spontaneously generated social demands is incompatible with the leading role of the party. The party, perpetually a vanguard, is seen as the only aggregator of social interests; the state is the party's handmaiden and its executive arm in the implementation of its tasks. Aiming at an eventual establishment of a perfect new society, the system is nevertheless well rooted in the soil of the traditional Russian culture, with its authoritarianism and messianic overtones.

Over time—1977 marked the sixtieth anniversary of the Russian Revolution—the party's program of social mobilization has indeed resulted in basic social and economic transformation. But no corresponding changes took place in the political system, the development of which had been arrested almost at inception. The failure to evolve popular consensus behind the mobilization program imposed from above in the quest for utopian ideological goals bred social alienation; at the same time new social forces, generated by the process, have begun to press for recognition and to demand participation. But instead of being accommodated, new demands have been met by emphasis on mobilization in perpetuity and on maintenance of political status quo. This preoccupation with system maintenance precluded all but a few efforts at system's perseverance, i.e., efforts to promote gradual adaptation aiming at long-term survival.[2] In fact, the maintenance of the system and of its cornerstone, the leading role of the Communist party, has all but replaced the original goal culture by becoming the final goal in itself. In Johnson's terminology this phenomenon is known as the transfer-goal culture.[3]

> A Communist party in power adopts a transfer culture, which it expounds and defends as moving society toward a utopian goal culture but which in fact has as its first two priorities the preservation of the party's power monopoly and the maintenance of the social system. Third in priority, but still of decisive importance, are schemes thought to be necessary for achieving the goal culture. . . . All three demand societal mobilization, a

process that is inevitably alienating because at least third priority goals have never been legitimized among the mass of the population.[4]

The Communist states of Eastern Europe, established some thirty years later, have inherited the Soviet model with its paradoxes and its ideological baggage. If anything, problems of change there are sharper than in the Soviet Union, because most East European countries had higher levels of economic development and civic culture than Russia had in 1917, and also because, with the exception of Yugoslavia and Albania, Communism was imposed there by Soviet military might and has been so maintained. Communist systems' incongruity with most national political cultures in the region adds up to the conflict between social pressures and the monopoly position of Communist parties.

Type, Scope, and Direction of Change

Analysis of the problems of change is complicated by the need to examine them over time and space.[5] In the case of the Soviet Union and Eastern Europe, the time span has been sixty and thirty years, respectively. For comparison purposes, the problem created by the time differential is more apparent than real, because Soviet experience has been telescoped in Eastern Europe, and in the seventies the development of the system was roughly at comparable levels throughout the region. The time factor, however, is meaningful in relation to the pattern of alternating periods of centralized control and relative relaxation. The pattern originates in the Soviet Union but has applied equally to all because of the Soviet hegemonic position. The Stalinist period of extreme control and centralization lasted until the dictator's death in 1953. The leadership of Nikita S. Khrushchev ushered in an era of relative relaxation marked by innovations and, in Eastern Europe, by considerable autonomy that, in turn, led to differentiation. It ended, in the Soviet Union, with Secretary

Khrushchev's ouster in 1964 and a return to partial re-Stalinization. In Eastern Europe the new control period began in 1968 with the suppression, by the Warsaw Pact forces, of the reforms in Czechoslovakia.

Problems of space are reflected in the variations—in size, geographic location, demographic and natural resource endowments, and political culture—between the Soviet Union and the states of East-Central Europe, and between East Europeans themselves. Feasibility of autarkic economic policies pursued in the Stalinist period, for example, was different in the Soviet Union, because of its size and resources, than it was in the small and resource-poor East European states. Similarly, a response to the party's monopoly control, when combined with the impact of modernization, has differed widely between societies with traditional authoritarian political cultures and societies with democratic or antiauthoritarian traditions.

An analysis of the process of change is also frequently colored by difficulties of definition as well as by effects of value judgment. It is frequently assumed, for example, that a change in Communist systems resulting from the impact of economic development must necessarily lead in the democratic direction and is seen as progressive, linear, and irreversible. Arising from the identification of the process of party-directed change with Western-type modernization (much of which was self-generated), the assumption rests on the ascription to the former of values commonly, if not always correctly, assigned to the latter.

In general, types of change may be classified by origin, nature, and direction. From the point of view of its *origin*, the key distinction is between an evolutionary (incremental) and a revolutionary change; from the point of view of its *nature*, between a qualitative and a quantitative change. A qualitative change involves a change in substance, in the very nature of the system, as defined by its principal features and characteristics. A quantitative change, on the other hand, may include far-reaching adaptations of structures, functions, or scope, or additions of new actors, but it stops short of affecting the system's basic nature.

All of the Communist societies came into being through revolutionary processes, either through revolution or by imposition from outside that amounted to a revolution, and their inception involved a qualitative change. Once established, however, the process of change within has been largely evolutionary and quantitative. This is not to say there were no attempts at revolutionary change. The abortive Hungarian Revolution of 1956 was suppressed because it aimed at the return to Western-style democracy, but near-revolutionary situations in Poland in 1956 and 1970 led to quantitative changes, the result of concessions designed to satisfy popular demands before they could lead to outbursts threatening the Communist system. In Czechoslovakia, the reforms of the Prague "Spring" culminated a process of incremental change. We shall never know whether the reform-induced pluralism, to which the Czechoslovak party attempted to adapt, would have led to its abdication of monopoly of power. Certainly, the judgment of the Soviet and other East European parties that dictated the Warsaw Pact invasion indicated the fear of exactly this kind of development.

But the outcomes, so far, of a similar type of incremental change in Yugoslavia, where no intervention has been feasible, would argue to the contrary. The scope of quantitative changes in that country has truly been enormous, but they have been confined within the basic mold of the system. The leading role exercised by the League of Communists of Yugoslavia (LCY) continues to be the cornerstone of the Yugoslav political system, even though it has been eroded by pluralist forces released by the implementation of workers' self-management and the decentralization of state and party structures. It can be argued, however, that a qualitative change did take place in the republics' position in the federation. The federal state structure now operates on the unanimity principle—each republic has a power of the veto—and the LCY appears to have been reduced to little more than a federation of independent parties held

together by the prestige, power, and charisma of President
Tito. The LCY nevertheless denies that it has been "federal-
ized" and insists that it is a unitary party of the Leninist type.
The change in the nature of the federation led neither to an
institutionalization of pluralism nor to the demise of ideology
as the basis of the legitimacy of the system, and the leading
party role has been reaffirmed with new vigor in the aftermath
of the 1971 Croat crisis. Despite this reaffirmation, the scope
and the depth of the Yugoslav reforms have gone far beyond
anything acceptable to the Soviet party. In contrast, the more
modest Hungarian economic reform has been acceptable, and
it has proved effective in meeting basic social needs at least in
part, even though pressures have lately been visible there for a
return to a more orthodox model.[6]

The *direction of change* cannot be assumed to be progressive
(i.e., responsive to social demands) in the case of Communist
regimes where spontaneously generated social demands do not
guarantee an appropriate positive political response. Rather, a
negative change may result in order to suppress or to neutralize
such demands. Thus *party-directed* and *society-directed*
change patterns, the one initiated from above, the other
generated from below, conflict more often than they complement one another. The first has predominated most clearly in
the initial period of consolidation and initiation of goal culture politics by each Communist regime, and in periods of
centralized control. The second has emerged in relaxation
periods and has prevailed then, providing no threat was discernible to system maintenance. But when such a threat has
been perceived by the leadership, concessions to popular
demands have been reversed in favor of the reassertion of the
party's leading role and its concomitant characteristics. As
social stimuli for change increase and the system "ages" for
want of meaningful adaptation, change in the face of popular
demands becomes increasingly difficult. Still, changes have
occurred with some regularity, involving the use of force in
extreme cases. It is paradoxical from the point of view of the
system that society-directed change, which would go far

towards the legitimation of Communist regimes, has had to be suppressed time and again because it posed a threat to the core of the system—the leading role of the Communist party. So far the direction of change has swung in a pendulumlike fashion between a progressive path reflecting social needs and demands and a regressive one seeking to reinforce characteristics of the system. Society-directed demands for change now pose a major dilemma for Communist leaders. If positive response is made, each concession will generate new and greater demands; if the demands are suppressed—as they must be eventually if system maintenance is to prevail—the costs, tangible and intangible, will be staggering. Finally, if there is no response, pent-up social frustrations that accumulate may lead to an outbreak of violence the consequences of which may be even worse.

Stimuli for Change

The process of change in Communist societies begins with initial social-mobilization policies dictated by the regimes' goal culture, the content of which has been broadly similar in all cases, and proceeds on an action-reaction continuum: The initial impact generates social reaction and new demands, which, in turn, evoke adjustment in policies, the impact of which is again felt in social reaction, and so on in a continuing process. Unlike the initial impact, however, the continuum is shaped and modified by each country's specific environment, which includes objective factors, such as size and resources, as well as subjective patterns of the values, attitudes, structures, and behavior characteristic of a particular national political culture. The broad variety in the spectrum of these variables in the region has been responsible for initial deviations from the Soviet model as well as for differential patterns of change that have emerged throughout the socialist community.

As the system matures, impulses for change multiply, when the momentum accelerates under the impact of key stimuli, internal and external. Modernization (in its Communist variant) and nationalism have been the two major internal stimuli for change. Added to it, since 1956, has been revisionism, as it has affected perceptions and behavior of the ruling elites. External stimuli have included the Soviet policy (for the East Europeans) and intrabloc relations, as well as the impact of the relations with the West. In the seventies the frequency of contacts within the bloc has intensified because of the newly launched policy of bloc integration.[7] Contacts with the West also accelerated massively under the impact of détente. The latter affected several broad areas: social and cultural behavior (in a return to interwar patterns) and economic policies influenced by trade exchanges and technology transfer. Demands for human rights accelerated notably in the aftermath of the Conference on Security and Cooperation in Europe (CSCE) held in Helsinki. In the realm of internal party relations, revisionism gained new strength from the proliferation of polycentrism in the world Communist movement; for the East European parties the development of Eurocommunism in particular has had important repercussions.

Volumes have been written on the relationship between modernization and political change in non-Communist as well as in Communist societies.[8] Specialists seem to agree that a higher degree of politicization is the inevitable outcome of modernization; the shift from the rural to the urban setting and accompanying role differentiation combine with access to mass education, communications, and services; social self-awareness is enhanced and stimulates expectations; and the demands are made for social self-fulfillment, the satisfaction of which requires greater participation in the political process. If political access is denied, frustrations accumulate, generating instability. Thus, a successful modernization model is assumed to include economic and social as well as political development (defined as an increase in per capita representation in the political process by which priorities are established[9]). The Communist variant of modernization, however, directed mobilization at a single goal—economic development—

relegating social development to a subsidiary role and totally ⌐
denying an opportunity for political development except in a
controlled environment. This created an imbalance, the
righting of which is now the object of social pressures as it is
reflected in the ongoing process of quantitative change.[10] If
Huntington is right that "the relationship between political
participation and political institutionalization determines the
stability of the political system,"[11] then the imbalance, unless
rectified, seriously threatens the stability of Communist
systems. Such rectification, however, is unlikely because the
subsystem autonomy of social groups is incompatible with the
Communist transfer culture, the maintenance of which is now
the key goal of the ruling elites.

In the politics of multiethnic societies, an enhanced ethnic
awareness has been a part of social politicization engendered by
modernization;[12] also, ethnicity has served increasingly as the
preferred base for interest articulation.[13] Both of these
observations are germane to the developments in the Soviet
Union, where the union republics—basic units comprising the
Soviet federation—have become aggregators of the interests of
their titular ethnic groups, and where the conflict between
dominant Russian nationalism and ethnic nationalisms of the
minorities now constitutes the major force for change and a
serious threat to the success of the Soviet Union's national
integration.[14] In contrast to the Soviet Union, Yugoslavia has
recognized and accommodated ethnicity, which has become the
motive power behind the Yugoslav reforms.[15] As noted
previously, the League of Communists of Yugoslavia is still a
Leninist and a unitary party de jure, but de facto it seems to be
an aggregate of six national parties. Despite, or perhaps
because of, the far-reaching accommodation of ethnic interests
in state and party structures, ethnic nationalism—Croat
separatism in particular—is still a major force that stands in
the way of Yugoslav national integration. The Slovak drive
for self-determination vis-à-vis Czech hegemony was one of

the main forces that contributed to the Prague "Spring"
reforms,[16] and it remains an important factor in postinvasion
Czechoslovakia.

In relations between the socialist states of Eastern Europe
and the Soviet Union, the impact of Communist mobilization
has only reinforced the particular nationalisms that had been
strong enough in the past to contribute to the disintegration of
the two empires and to be reflected in the post–World War I
Versailles settlement. In Eastern Europe in general, in contrast
to Asia, nationalism has proved to be extremely dysfunctional
to the establishment and maintenance of Communist systems
because Communism, identified with Russia, evokes traditional Russophobia in all but two East European countries
(Bulgaria and Czechoslovakia). In all cases, nationalism has
affected ruling elites as much as the societies at large, and each
of the parties has made attempts to legitimize itself through
espousal of national interests and national traditions.

Building socialism within the framework of national
interest and at the expense of "proletarian internationalism"
was first essayed by the Communist Party of the Soviet Union
(CPSU) and has been a source of conflict between it and other
parties ever since the early days of the Comintern. In Eastern
Europe national Communism was pioneered by the LCY, the
example followed overtly by Albanian and Romanian parties,
covertly by all others. Within the world Communist movement, latent party nationalism erupted into polycentrism in
the wake of the Sino-Soviet quarrel, and, with Eurocommunism, the impact of "national deviation" is again on the increase in Eastern Europe. For the CPSU there is basic conflict
in its coincident espousal of "proletarian internationalism"
and imperial "Soviet patriotism." Policies functional in one
area tend to be highly counterproductive in another, their
simultaneous pursuit opening up loopholes for the assertion of
autonomous interests by all subordinate actors involved: in
domestic politics, in relations within the bloc and with the
ruling parties outside, in relations with the nonruling parties,

and in relations with decolonization forces in the Third World
that the CPSU attempts to control. For example, the emphasis
on national self-determination for the Third World fuels
feelings of ethnicity at home; concessions made to Eurocom-
munists and to Yugoslavia in the interest of a (largely illusory)
Communist unity in Europe immediately reverberate in
Eastern Europe, where they are picked up in support of
independent policies—with alacrity by Romania's Ceausescu,
with caution by Hungary's Kádár or Poland's Gierek. Attempts
to foster the integration of Eastern Europe and the Soviet
Union are welcomed on the Soviet domestic scene because
of the opportunities they offer for an increase in the republics' autonomy; they are resented in Eastern Europe for exactly
the opposite reasons and looked at with suspicion by Euro-
communists. As a force for change, however, nationalism in
itself does not carry the seeds of democratic reforms, and
in most cases it has been perfectly compatible with the maintenance of the leading role of the party. A democratic element
appears in nationalism-stimulated change only when the particular national political culture has strong democratic, antiauthoritarian components. Only in these circumstances has the
drive for national self-determination strengthened pressures
for political pluralism generated by modernization. This type
of conjunction, highly dysfunctional to Communist-system
maintenance, has occurred in Czechoslovakia and Poland; it is
visible also in the Soviet Baltic Republics.[17]

Revisionism became a force for change only in the aftermath
of (in Carl Linden's phrase) Khrushchev's 1956 "Iconoclasm."[18] By discrediting Stalin and with him the myth of the
infallibility of the party, Khrushchev had shaken, in many
cases shattered, the members' faith in the movement and
validated their hidden doubts about the discrepancy between
the system's claims and social reality. Thus the search for new
solutions, going back to the "scriptures" themselves, sometimes beyond, was not only stimulated but also legitimated. For
the ruling elites the search cannot really extend beyond

Leninism because they have to cling to the "vanguard" concept in the interests of self-preservation; others are less constrained and have been offering a range of alternative roads to socialism on a broad left-to-right spectrum.[19] New currents of change stimulated by the revisionists have been visible particularly among the reformers of the Czechoslovak "Spring," the Praxis group in Yugoslavia (now denied the forum of publication and free discussion), and various groups in Poland and Hungary, as well as individuals elsewhere.

Turning now to external stimuli, the impact of Soviet policies in Eastern Europe has obviously been enormous—and in the event of a conflict decisive—because of the asymmetrical power of the Soviet Union and East European states. Having established Communist systems in the region, the Soviets have been opposed to change within the bloc although some innovations acceptable to the Soviet Union and experimentation prompted by local needs have been tolerated. The problem appears to be not only to establish general parameters of permissible change, but also to prevent "infection" across national boundaries within the bloc by containing undesirable developments in the country of their origin. It is tacitly understood, for example, that some countries—Poland, Hungary, and for a time Czechoslovakia in domestic politics, and Romania in external relations—can get away with policies that are not tolerable elsewhere. A technique of isolating the phenomenon on the grounds of national peculiarities—such as the decollectivization of agriculture and the autonomy of the Roman Catholic Church in Poland or the socialist market in Hungary—has been reasonably effective. But a spread of "bourgeois" or "nationalist" deviations is extremely difficult to contain, as demonstrated in 1956 and 1968. Moreover, the diffusion has been significantly maximized in the seventies because of integration policies.

The seepage of innovations between Eastern Europe and the Soviet Union has occurred in both directions. Zvi Gitelman writes that "East European political systems are often seen as change agents influencing the Soviet system, and generally in a 'liberalizing' direction."[20] He also discusses three case studies of innovation diffusion, those of Yugoslavia, Czecho-slovakia, and Hungary, and assesses their impact on Soviet domestic politics.[21] Equally interesting may be an attempt to trace East European impact on the growth of ethnic nationalism in the Soviet Union such as that in the Ukraine at the time of the Prague "Spring," or the influence Polish strikers might have had on the demands made in Moscow in 1978 by a group of trade unionists.[22]

At the same time some negative patterns of social behavior characteristic of Soviet society seem to have taken root in Eastern Europe, as reflected by absenteeism, corruption, poor work habits, drunkenness, and mass social alienation evidenced by indifference to political life and attempts at feathering one's own nest. The Soviet Union carefully watches the winds of change and, as is well known, has been instrumental in arresting and reversing patterns it considers dangerous for system maintenance. But the Soviets' external parameters of change have not always been clear and thus have allowed for considerable latitude. Since 1968, however, while stimuli for change have multiplied, the parameters appear to be more constricted, implying an even more negative attitude towards change. A new test case may be shaping up in Poland if the trends developing there since 1975 continue.[23]

The impact of the West, on the other hand, has been positive in stimulating new currents of change, whether by direct contact, by persuasion, or by example. Indeed, it is because the policy of détente is considered to carry a contagious virus of democratic change that it has been denounced by the conservative elements within the CPSU and other ruling parties, despite its manifold advantages to the Soviet bloc. The transfer of technology from West to East has been one of the main reasons for the policy of détente on the Soviet side.

Technology is of vital importance if the economies of the bloc countries are to negotiate successfully the transition from an extensive to an intensive growth pattern, thereby restimulating their declining rates of growth. But along with the desired tools and processes come action patterns and market characteristics incompatible with the command planning system that may stimulate forces impossible to contain. Avenues of possible change generated by implants of Western technology are explored elsewhere in this book.[24]

Under the policy of détente, East-West exchanges, political and cultural as well as economic, have served to breach the Iron Curtain of the Stalinist era and to open the region anew to Western influence. This has been particularly important in the case of Eastern Europe, where traditional pro-Western orientation has revived, reinforcing Western political culture patterns and forces of pluralism. The human rights factor in particular, a by-product of the CSCE Helsinki agreement and its follow-up conferences, has given new respectability to social group demands for the free exercise of civil rights and freedom of expression and for participation in the political process. As a result of this growing concern for human rights, the Soviet and East European dissident movements, once purely domestic, are now of international interest. This has been reinforced by the emphasis the new Carter administration has placed on human rights as part of U.S. foreign policy. None of the ruling bloc parties has been willing to admit officially any outside interference in the matter of their dissidents, but repressing them has become increasingly inconvenient. Although dissident movements and their demands are growing, given a new lease on life because of international legitimacy and the hesitancy of the home governments to crack down on them, this has occurred more in Eastern Europe than in the Soviet Union, where the movement faces attrition because of selective arrests and the exile of successive leaders.

Within the leadership and rank and file of Communist

parties of Eastern Europe, the inroads made by Eurocommunism have reinforced those made by polycentrism earlier. Contacts between parties are stimulated by the Soviet insistence on the forging of a new common Communist front in Europe. Felt primarily in its support for each party's national sovereignty, Eurocommunism also enhances pressures for pluralism. The three Western parties' theoretical acceptance of parliamentary democracy and pluralism is a powerful stimulus to Communist would-be reformers who believe that socialism "with a human face" is in the realm of possibilities.

Perspectives for Change: The Demands and the Constraints

It was argued earlier that only a quantitative type of change has been allowed to evolve in Communist systems and that economic and social development has not been accompanied by an appropriate political change, thus creating an imbalance the redress of which is increasingly more pressing. In other words, it appears that the more mature Communist systems are reaching an impasse, a conflict between the society and the system, that can be resolved only by a revolutionary upheaval or at the least a compromise that ultimately may require abdication of power by the ruling elite, a prospect unlikely at present since the system's basic principles have been reaffirmed by all of the ruling parties. The questions to be examined, therefore, are:

First: what are these basic principles, why and to what extent are they threatened, and where are the pressures felt most acutely?

Second: is it possible to resolve the conflict through evolutionary quantitative change within the parameters of the system, or is the system basically incapable of accommodating it? The following discussion attempts to analyze these questions and to provide some tentative answers.

The basic principle of any Communist system is *the leading*

role of the party in society, a change in which would mean the
establishment of a different type of political system altogether.
The concept is derived from Lenin rather than from Marx and
to be implemented requires the simultaneous presence of
three conditions:

1. Party control of political power, which means having a
   monopoly to aggregate all social interests as well as the
   power to assign social priorities and to control their
   implementation by any means, including the use of
   terror.
2. The legitimation of the party's power monopoly
   through the Leninist vanguard theory, which requires
   the maintenance of Marxist-Leninist ideology as the
   system's secular religion. This is codified in the
   "scriptures" that can be interpreted (infallibly) only by
   the party's leaders. The legitimizing role of the ideology
   requires that the party also monopolize communications.
3. The application of the principle of democratic centralism to the total range of social relations. This implies a
   system of command from the top complemented by
   unconditional obedience from below. As practiced in
   Communist systems, the democratic aspects of this
   principle—election of the higher by the lower bodies,
   and reporting by the former to the latter—have served the
   purposes of support building and socialization and do
   not imply any responsibility to listen to the "electorate"
   below. The principle governs intraparty relations as it
   does public administration and the activities of all social
   organizations. In economic management it is expressed
   in the command planning system.

Most spontaneous social pressures in mature Communist
systems challenge the leading role of the party either in toto or
in one of its aspects. The challenge has been felt most strongly
in the area of interest articulation—social groups demanding

the right to exist and to organize, and the right to participate in policy process through institutionalized channels. Recognition here would mean legitimation of subsystem autonomy as well as the party's abdication of its claim to be the sole aggregator of social interests, leading ultimately to a multi-party system. Milovan Djilas and the Czech reformers recognized this as the ultimate outcome of the pluralization process. Demands for interest articulation exist not only in the society at large but also within the bureaucracies and the party itself. As Johnson notes:

> Despite the fact that Communist transfer-culture doctrine rejects the right of autonomous groups to develop or articulate interests distinct from those of the party, the Communist mobilization regime slowly generates autonomous groups within the party leadership.[25]

Interest articulation and access to decision making are incompatible with the principle of the party's power monopoly as well as with the principle of democratic centralism; it also violates ideological assumptions of the absence of social conflict within a socialist state with its, by definition, nonantagonistic classes. Moreover, concessions in this area threaten the very survival of the ruling elite, as has been demonstrated in Czechoslovakia and Yugoslavia.

Pressures for economic reforms, particularly for decentralization of the planning process and for recognition of market elements in economic management and production, are closely related to the general area of interest articulation and stem from the same causes. There is a difference here, however. The need for reform is recognized by the ruling elites because they want to improve economic performance in order to maintain the system by both competing successfully with the capitalists and meeting growing consumer demands.

Another major area of social demand has been that of freedom of expression, to be protected by the rule of law and curtailment of the terror apparatus by placing it under the law. Pressures in this area contradict directly the core assumptions of the ideology and the power requirements of the ruling elites. Freedom of expression challenges the party's monopoly of communications; the rule-of-law principle negates the Marxist concept of the superstructure whereby the law (and all other social institutions) is a product of the economic base and a tool of the ruling class.

Attempts to cope with social conflict generated by pressures for change illustrate the basic inability of the system to adapt, if the price is the loss by the party of its leading role. But at the same time they show that within basic constraints there is considerable room for adjustment. In his pioneering book, Chalmers Johnson[26] recognizes four distinct areas where change has, to a greater or lesser degree, taken place. These include structures, freedom of expression and the rule of law, economic management, and the relationship between the Soviet Union and those countries upon which it has externally imposed the Communist system. All of these changes fall within the limits of quantitative change, as defined previously. It may be useful to examine developments in each area more closely.

Examples of changes in structures (society-directed as well as party-directed) have been both numerous and far-reaching, if one includes also the area of economic management. Structural tinkering may be explained, in part, by a certain propensity of the system to rely on the human element (the "man controls nature" assumption), as well as to perceive administrative manipulation as a cure-all in dealing with problems, regardless of whether or not they are related to human or administrative causes. Bureaucratization represents one aspect of structural change. It reflects the system's reliance on executive instruments and has also served to divert group demands into channels that reinforce, rather than threaten, system maintenance by giving the most important of them a vested interest in the system. Bureaucratization of interests in Communist systems has been so pronounced that analysts have come to identify major interest groups with key bureaucracies or their branches,[27] in contrast to the prevalent Western concept of pressure groups of an associational nature.[28] Thus the elites that play an identifiable role in Communist policy process include among others *apparatchiki* (members of the party apparatus), security police, the military, and industrial managers; their interests are articulated by appropriate bureaucracies and aggregated, at the top leadership level, by the party. The success of these diversionary tactics is illustrated by the resistance to economic reforms of the very people that should be most interested in their promotion: industrial managers and middle-level state and party bureaucrats—reform would mean a new, unfamiliar, and insecure setting for them to cope with. On the whole institutional pressure groups (the in-groups) have vested interests in the preservation of the status quo and are therefore opposed to any reforms that may threaten it. But they support reforms that are likely to enhance the system's efficiency, especially in economic performance.

Social groups other than those identified with the bureaucratic structures are the out-groups, deprived of direct access to policymaking and unable legally to organize, although they are nominally represented by a multitude of party-directed social organizations known as "transmission belts." The out-groups have been most troublesome to the ruling elites because their accumulating frustrations and alienation adversely affect the performance of the system and introduce a threat to its long-range stability. The search for a formula that would accommodate such pressures without prejudice to the principle of the leading role of the party has led to a whole range of experimental innovations. Techniques tried with varying degrees of success have included a partial transformation of "transmission belts" into genuine interest articulators, a co-optation of technocrats into the ruling elites, an institutionalization of consultation with professional elites, and last but not least, an emphasis on "participation by the masses" in the activities of social and political organizations.

A gradual transformation of "transmission belts" into

semiassociational (but still under the guidance of the party) groups took place on a rather broad scale in Yugoslavia; but within the bloc only Hungarian trade unions can be listed in this category, although inroads may have been made elsewhere. More common by far have been the techniques of co-optation and consultation as applied to technical and professional elites. Co-optation into the party power elite has been used successfully in the case of the technocrats, particularly in East Germany,[29] but the practice has been followed also in the Soviet Union and other East European countries. Consultation is now becoming a standard technique; it opens up channels of communication to a much wider range of professional groups, including economists, lawyers and educators (in the Soviet Union and Eastern Europe), sociologists (in Eastern Europe, particularly in Poland, Hungary, and preinvasion Czechoslovakia), and others. In each case expert opinion is sought by party decision makers in the interest of greater efficiency either by setting up special think tanks—Moscow's Institute of World Economics and International Relations (IMEMO) and Institute of the United States and Canada are two well-known examples—or by opening up an issue for a public debate in preparation for reform.

All of these innovations, however, leave unrepresented the broadest and most restive social interests, identified by generic class designation, such as workers, peasants, students and youth in general, and the creative intelligentsia. It is the "mass participation" technique—going through the motions of attendance, discussion, and voting at innumerable meetings, conferences, and sessions carefully orchestrated by the party— that is designed to take care of these groups' political self-fulfillment. In scope it ranges from participation in meetings at one's place of work or an appropriate social organization to participation in the work of elective territorial assemblies (if one is an elected deputy) or party organizations (if one is a member of the rank and file). Depending on a given system's degree of quantitative evolution, party control of the participation process ranges from open and total to covert and minimal, but even in the latter case is still adequate to keep spontaneity in check. Controlled participation has always been seen as crucial for purposes of political socialization, but in the sixties and seventies it has acquired a new importance as a palliative in meeting the demands for free political participation, and the emphasis on it has markedly increased. By and large, however, it has failed to serve as an adequate substitute for true participation and has instead contributed further to political frustration and the sense of alienation between the rulers and the ruled.

Composition and structure of leadership also has been subject to change, as noted by Johnson, and reorganization of key bureaucracies is a common occurrence. In the Soviet Union it was characteristic particularly of the Khrushchev period. In general, few of these changes seem to have been of a permanent nature; most reflect either a power configuration or an attempt to deal with a particular problem. Leadership succession continues to be noninstitutionalized, and leadership change in most cases is a result of an upheaval and/or an occasion for a power struggle.[30] This results in party leadership alternating between one-man ascendancy and collective rule, reflecting on the one hand the bureaucratization of key interest groups that favor collective leadership, and on the other the dynamics of the system that encourages competition for supreme power among top leaders. Khrushchev's efforts at partial institutionalization of the composition of leading party bodies[31] were revoked by his successors[32] as were most of his other structural reforms, including the CPSU's "bifurcation." In the seventies most of the East European parties (except in Poland and in Hungary) merged the positions of the head of state (presidency) and the head of the party so that the real and the formal top power positions would be represented by one man—a practice followed also by the Soviet Union under the new 1977 (Brezhnev) constitution, probably for reasons of prestige and convenience, particularly when dealing with the West.

Structural changes also reflect efforts at streamlining management, thus facilitating control from the top and strengthening the leading role of the party. Local government reforms in Romania (in 1968-69) and in Poland (in 1972 and 1975) are an example. Both eliminated superfluous links in local administration and increased the number while reducing the size of key units of territorial administration. At the same time in both countries the posts of state and party chiefs were merged and placed in the hands of one man. In the words of one expert, two major goals were thus accomplished:

> The reforms eliminated the possibility of conflict in key positions throughout the political system by creating new executive posts that combined the party and governmental positions previously held by different individuals; and they strengthened the position of the top leader by expanding the number of these posts, thus reducing the authority of provincial leaders who might present a threat to the center.[33]

Attempts at economic reform are too well known to be restated here.[35] Two points should be made, however. One is that even in market-type reforms, with indicative rather than command planning and decentralized economic management (as in the case of Yugoslavia and to a lesser extent in Hungary), the "commanding heights" have remained, however tenuously, in the hands of the party. The other is that, after the Czech debacle, the preferred pattern of reform within the bloc is that of a recentralized East German variant, which leaves intact the command planning system and presents no threat to system maintenance. But its economic effectiveness in solving the region's problems is minimal. If fully implemented, this Soviet preference which has found expression also in the policies of the Council for Mutual Economic Assistance (CMEA), places in jeopardy the deviant pattern of the Hungarian New Economic Mechanism.[36]

Reforms in Johnson's second area of change, freedom of expression and the rule of law, are almost nonexistent. Policies in this area have been characterized also by the pendulum effect: periods of relative relaxation alternating with periods of repression. The use of terror has largely been supplanted by persuasion, but its apparatus remains intact throughout the bloc (including Yugoslavia) and is still utilized when needed, the Helsinki Conference and its provisions notwithstanding. While there is more emphasis on "socialist legality" and on the conformity of official actions to it, the fountainhead of law (i.e., the will of the party) and the conception of its role in society (i.e., the tool of the ruling class) have not been altered in any way. Neither has the role of ideology as the legitimizer of the system. Most observers agree that few, if any, dedicated believers still survive among the ruling elites, but no substitute has yet been found for ideology in justifying the party's hold on power.[34] A degree of de-ideologization has followed a new trend towards pragmatic policymaking, but all of the Communist regimes continue to stress ideological myths and to justify policies in ideological terms. As to what degree, the less legitimacy a regime has in the society, the more shrill, it seems, are its invocations of ideological sanctions.

The last important area of change to be considered is that of relations between the Soviet Union and the Communist states established and supported by it. Here the pendulum effect is visible again in alternate periods of control and relaxation. Pressures for emancipation from Soviet tutelage, it should be noted, do not challenge any of the systemic imperatives, unless such an emancipation is coupled also with internal liberalization. The main challenge here is to the Soviet hegemony. Both are equally nonacceptable to the CPSU, however. An effort to maximize control that has characterized Soviet policy vis-à-vis Eastern Europe since 1968 has been reflected in the policy of integration of the CMEA-WTO (Warsaw Treaty Organization) group under the Soviet aegis. But the Soviet approach is both more flexible and more realistic than it was under Stalin, and, as previously discussed, it leaves considerable latitude in the degree of autonomy permitted.[37] Overall, the degree of autonomy either in foreign policy (Romania) or in internal affairs (Hungary, Poland, preinvasion Czechoslovakia) depends, it seems, on outcomes of a cost-benefit analysis in any given case. Main factors considered include damage versus nuisance value of the deviation, the danger of "infection" elsewhere in the bloc, the danger of an explosion if enforcement is tried, and the feasibility of an invasion and its probable aftereffects at home and abroad.

Nationalism threatens stability of multiethnic societies, where pressures for ethnic autonomy may easily be converted into separatism. In bloc relations it has been the major stimulus behind the satellite-to-client transition, posing a constant threat to Soviet hegemony in the region. It is also a major obstacle to plans for regional integration and a continuous source of conflict between bloc members.

Conclusion

In the final analysis one cannot assume either the institutionalization of change patterns in Communist systems or their irreversible character. Far-reaching as the evolution has been in some countries, it has not affected the party's sacerdotal claims, or the exercise of its leading role as the ultimate aggregator of social interests and as the ultimate interpreter and enforcer of reality. The practice of democratic centralism has been eroded by some important innovations; but no matter how extensive, the reforms have remained a matter of privilege rather than right, to be granted or revoked by the ruling elites as long as their hold on power is intact. Clearly, qualitative change through evolution is not possible because the ruling elite controls the process of decision making and will not acquiesce in its own demise.

Consequently, the answer to the second question is that the system is basically incapable of adapting to a democratic-type challenge. Whether or not social pressures within the system take a democratic path is a function of the system's "maturity" and of the type and intensity of the stimuli for change. Primarily, however, it is the function of the congruity between the system and a given political culture because the culture shapes the response to all stimuli. While modernization does generate group demands for recognition and participation, not all such demands necessarily lead to pluralism. It appears that the more authoritarian the political culture, the fewer demands there are for basic changes and the easier it is to accommodate new forces within the old structures. But if democratic elements exist in a political culture, they reinforce the democratic impact of modernization to form a highly explosive political mix, especially when the two are further strengthened by nationalism.

If this is so, then the theory of conflict between society-directed pressures for democratic change and the Communist system should be amended. In societies where political culture is congruous with the system, as in the Soviet Union, East Germany, or Bulgaria, such a conflict does not pose an immediate threat to political stability even when modernization levels are high. Conversely, when basic incongruity exists between the political culture and the system, as in Czechoslovakia, Poland, or Hungary, especially if reinforced by modernizing pressures, such a conflict breeds demands for democratization and generates instability leading to revolutionary situations.

Notes

1. Chalmers Johnson, "Comparing Communist Nations" in Chalmers Johnson, ed. *Change in Communist Systems* (Stanford, 1970), pp. 1-32.
2. See the discussion in Zvi Gitelman, *Beyond Leninism: Political Development in Eastern Europe* (Pittsburgh, 1971), p. 1.
3. Johnson, *Communist Systems*, p. 25.
4. Ibid.
5. Samuel P. Huntington, "The Change to Change," *Compara-*

tive Politics (January 1971), p. 285.

6. See Arpad Abonyi and Ivan I. Sylvain, "The Impact of CMEA Integration on Social Change in East Europe: The Case of Hungary's New Economic Mechanism," this volume.

7. See Teresa Rakowska-Harmstone, "Socialist Internationalism and Eastern Europe—A New Stage," *Survey* (Winter 1976), pp. 38-54, and "Socialist Internationalism—Part II," ibid. (Spring 1976), pp. 81-86.

8. See, for example, Karl W. Deutsch, "Social Mobilization and Political Development," *American Political Science Review* (September 1961), and Jason L. Finkle and Richard W. Gable, *Political Development and Social Change* (New York, 1966), for general works; and Johnson, *Communist Systems,* and Mark Field, ed., *Social Consequences of Modernization in Communist Societies* (Baltimore, 1976), for Communist societies.

9. Johnson, *Communist Systems,* p. 13. Johnson also defines economic development as the increase in per capita productivity, and social development as the increase in per capita level of living and access to means of social self-fulfillment.

10. Ibid, p. 14.

11. Huntington, "Change to Change," p. 314.

12. Karl W. Deutsch, *Nationalism and Social Communication* (Cambridge, Mass., 1963), pp. 81-106.

13. Nathan Glazer and Daniel P. Moynihan, eds., Introduction to *Ethnicity, Theory and Experience* (Cambridge, Mass., 1975), p. 7.

14. Teresa Rakowska-Harmstone, "Ethnicity and Change in the Soviet Union"; this volume.

15.Gary W. Bertsch, "Ethnicity and Politics in Ethnic Yugoslavia," ibid., pp. 88-99. See also Bertsch, "Participation, Change, and Stability: Yugoslavia in Comparative Perspective," this volume.

16. Stanislaw J. Kirschbaum, "National Self-Assertion in Slovakia," George W. Simmonds, ed., *Nationalism in the USSR and Eastern Europe in the Era of Brezhnev and Kosygin* (Detroit, Mich., 1977), pp. 380-400.

17. Simmonds, *Nationalism,* sections on Estonia, Latvia, and Lithuania, pp. 116-87.

18. See Carl A. Linden, "Marxism-Leninism, Systemic Legitimacy, and Political Culture," this volume.

19. See Gitelman, *Beyond Leninism,* pp. 23-29.

20. Zvi Y. Gitelman, *The Diffusion of Political Innovation: From Eastern Europe to the Soviet Union* (Sage Publications, 1972), p. 5. For the discussion of diffusion of innovation in the bloc, see also Richard V. Burks, *Technological Innovation and Political Change*

in Communist Eastern Europe, RAND Memorandum RM 6051-PR (Santa Monica, Calif.); and Andrew Gyorgy and James A. Kuhlman, eds., *Innovation in Communist Systems* (Boulder, Co., 1978).

21. Gitelman, *Political Innovation*, pp. 33-53.

22. *Manchester Guardian Weekly*, March 12, 1978.

23. An emergence of openly organized (if illegal) groups of political opposition—at least four separate organizations with units in all major cities—and of open *samizdat* in Poland, followed the workers food riots of June 1976. See Jan Gross, "Crisis Management in Poland," this volume.

24. See John P. Hardt, "Imperatives of Economic Reform and Communist Political Systems," this volume.

25. Johnson, *Communist Systems*, p. 17.

26. Ibid., p. 3.

27. See, for example, H.G. Skilling and F. Griffiths, eds., *Interest Groups in Soviet Politics* (Princeton, N.J., 1973).

28. In the Almond and Powell terminology, interest groups in communist societies can be classified as "institutional" rather than "associational." See Gabriel A. Almond and G. Bingham Powell, Jr., *Comparative Politics: A Developmental Approach* (Boston, 1966), pp. 77-78.

29. See Thomas A. Baylis, *The Technical Intelligentsia and the East German Elite* (Berkeley, Calif., 1974); and Peter C. Ludz, *The Changing Party Elite in East Germany* (Cambridge, Mass., 1968).

30. See Myron Rush, *Political Succession in Communist Regimes* (Ithaca, N.Y., 1976); and Andrzej Korbonski, "Leadership Succession and Political Change in Eastern Europe," *Studies in Comparative Communism* (Spring-Summer 1976), pp. 3-26.

31. See *Current Soviet Policies* IV (Bloomington, Ind.), p. 204.

32. See *Current Soviet Policies* V (Bloomington, Ind.), p. 159.

33. Korbonski, *Comparative Communism*, p. 16.

34. See Linden, "Marxism-Leninism," this volume.

35. For a recent comprehensive treatment see H.H. Höhman, M.C. Kaser, and K.C. Thalheim, eds., *The New Economic Systems of Eastern Europe* (Berkeley, Calif., 1975).

36. See Abonyi and Sylvain, "The Impact of CMEA Integration on Social Change in Eastern Europe," this volume.

37. As Robin A. Remington points out in *The Warsaw Pact: Case Studies in Communist Conflict Resolution* (Cambridge, Mass., 1971), in its evolution the Warsaw Treaty Organization has provided an institutional framework for the adjustment of conflicts between member states.

2
Marxism-Leninism: Systemic Legitimacy and Political Culture

Carl A. Linden

A perennial question among students of Soviet affairs is "What role does the Marxist-Leninist doctrine of the Communist party rulership play in the Soviet system?" Out of their often complex debate over the past half-century or so, two broad schools of thought emerge. One school sees the doctrine as the inner rationale of the system and identifies basic interconnections between the doctrine's teachings and the conduct of the leadership over its history. It discerns consistency in the combination of Marxism's secularized messianic purpose (i.e., Communism) and Leninism's method of revolutionary realpolitik to accomplish that purpose—the first element reinforces the second and the second is an extreme expression and elaboration of the precept that the end justifies the means. The party leadership, according to this view, sees itself as engaged in a self-fulfilling project. The other school, by contrast, sees in the doctrine and its application something of a grand rationalization of the rule of a power group and points to apparent inconsistencies between what the power group preaches and what it practices and contradiction between ends it proclaims and means it employs in ruling the country. The sense of the term "rationalization" here is roughly the psychological one, namely, the use of a rational explanation of behavior to disguise motives whose reasons are other than those presented in the explanation. The explanation, in this case, is

Marxism-Leninism as the leadership presents it both to the outside world and to itself.

On either account, one thing seems clear. Whether the Marxist-Leninist ideology is a rationale or rationalization, without it the rulership would not remain what it is; it would become something else. If those guiding the party-state collectively and at a stroke suffered loss of belief in the doctrine, doctrinal amnesia, it is most doubtful that they would or could continue to conduct themselves as before—no more than, say, a mental patient freed of an obsession is the same as he was, nor more than someone who no longer accepts the reasons that sustained his past actions remains as he was.

The suggestion that the sway of Marxism-Leninism over the Soviet rulership may be compared to an obsessive state of mind is not so farfetched. A striking thing about Marxism-Leninism is that it seeks to justify itself *both* as a final rationale of human action as such and a rationalization of specific actions. On the one hand, it presents itself as the bearer of an ultimate knowledge of the world and its future that informs its action and, on the other, it characterizes itself as an "ideology." In Marxist terms an ideology is always a kind of rationalization and something less than the whole truth—though related to the behavior of a class, not of an individual, to be sure. That is to say, it knows itself to be *opinion* and not full knowledge. In this case, it sees itself as the rationalization of the self-interested motives of the proletariat as a class in its drive for power, or at least of those who assume leadership in its name. It thus involves itself in a kind of cunning self-deception, which, when pressed, it will admit. However, in its admission it also insists that of all ideologies it is the one *true* deception serving a yet unrevealed truth—a valid deception in the tradition of the necessary myth or noble lie. This double view of itself resembles that peculiar self-awareness of some obsessive-compulsives regarding the method in their madness.

In fact, it perhaps is just this peculiar combining of rationale and rationalization in the doctrine that gives it and the behavior of its adherents an obsessive quality. The rationale is not just a concept whose truth is received in the quiet of reason as a mathematician accepts the proof of a theorem on principles of logic alone, but rather an idea that places its adherent under a total compulsion to obey its demand in all spheres of life. As a result the Marxist-Leninist, like the obsessed, displays a peculiar single-mindedness in grappling with the outside world. The rationale precisely permits him to rationalize or justify actions that otherwise are doubtful or unacceptable in terms of most common notions of ethics or moralities both political and private. In the case of the Soviet leadership, these characteristics have been manifest over its history in its persistent and repeated application of force and ready expenditure of vast human energies in the name of the doctrine despite staggering human costs and deprivations. Like an obsession, Marxism-Leninism provides a totalistic explanation of the human life situation and also inclines its adherents to go to extreme lengths in resisting any questioning of its premises by others. In the Soviet case this tendency is reflected in the rulership's practice of treating any and all criticism of its orthodoxy not as normal political challenges answerable by the usual political methods of civil society but as subversion necessitating suppression.

The obsession analogy does not apply so well to the beliefs and behavior of political men in other systems whose public orthodoxies are not totalist. Such political men, by contrast, often display psychological tolerance of ideological challenge and even seem able to have one or another element of their views of the world undercut without themselves undergoing serious psychological change. The analogy does, however, apply to the Soviet politcal command to such a degree that it might even be said that Marxism-Leninism is the obsession of the systemic "soul" of the party-state. This does not mean that all or even most of the subjects of the party-state need be "true believers." Those who direct and sustain its command structure, however, should be believers for any disbelief among them, it must be recognized, endangers the system's vitality.

Again pursuing the analogy, one might imagine a maximum security psychiatric hospital isolated from the outside world. Further, imagine that a coterie of sophisticated intruders suffering from the same obsession have successfully substituted themselves for the medical directorate. All the patients and lesser personnel of the hospital—except for perhaps a few brave souls—find themselves strongly compelled to go along with and humor the obsession of their controllers. Many of those who are less than true believers over time rise to leading positions as they more or less successfully absorb or simulate the obsession as the necessary precondition of self-preservation and advancement in the system. Many, if not most, of the inmates will suspect something is not quite right in the institution. The obsessed themselves will strive to remove the source of trouble from the viewpoint the obsession rigorously imposes upon them. They will war against open opponents of the obsession's claims outside their ranks but will be especially disturbed about secret enemies within their ranks and will strive to ferret them out. Others may begin, however, to question the obsessive directorship itself, imputing error and abuses to it. As a result, the obsession itself may come indirectly under question. Moves to revise its view of the world so as to avert some of its more baneful practical consequences will be attempted. Yet as the danger that the obsession and its systematic direction of the life of the hospital will be undermined grows, those who have been reared under its sway and have risen to power and position on its basis will react to prevent its destruction. Some will do this because they are obsessed themselves; others, because they fear the practical outcome of the revisionary moves. But once the revisionist challenge has been made, the hold of the obsession on the inmates will no longer be quite what it was. The protégés of the first obsessed directors who now find themselves in charge will seek to preserve their grip and the obsession's weakened hold through certain grudging compromises with the changed reality, hoping the hidden crisis in the institution's affairs will pass. As may be apparent, the obsession analogy has been used to describe the phases of Soviet history from Lenin and his Bolsheviks through Stalin and Khrushchev to Brezhnev.

Analogies, of course, have their limitations. Marxism-Leninism is something more than an obsessive state of a collective psyche, though in some of its key characteristics, especially in its institutionalized forms, it has been shown to be not unlike such a state. Marxism-Leninism provides the rationale not only of leadership action, but also of the governing system that action has brought into being. While the doctrine is essential to the existence of that system, it is also in another aspect a part of that larger system. The doctrine has become incorporated into the party-state. Lenin described this ideological institutionalization by drawing a distinction between his notion of an "organized party" as against a party that is only a loose grouping of people linked by a shared ideology. The "organized party," in his view, implies the establishment of authority, the transformation of the power of ideas into the power of authority, the subordination of lower party bodies to higher party bodies. Here Lenin was opposing his notion of organization to the less rigid view of the more moderate wing of Russian Marxists in his conflict with them in the first few years of this century. Although in the above passage Lenin was referring only to the party that his concept of ideas would become, the authority of his "ideocracy" would later infuse the party-ruled Soviet state or the Soviet party-state that emerged out of the Bolshevik seizure of power in Russia in 1917.

The "state" of the party-state arises out of the Bolshevik capture in October 1917 of the self-governing workers councils, or "soviets," in Moscow and Petrograd (later Leningrad). The soviets had formed more or less spontaneously out of the Russian revolutions of 1905 and 1917, quite independently of the leadership of Lenin's small Bolshevik faction. Lenin entered upon the scene and exploited the soviets as a crucial symbol of popular revolutionary legitimacy for his party, while at the same time suppressing these bodies as the autonomous and authentic expressions they had been of the broader popular revolution. The bare image of the original substance of the workers soviets of the 1917 revolution is retained in the present "Soviet" state in the bare name and in the powerless and ceremonial hierarchy of soviets culminating in the present day Supreme Soviet. The ideocratic principle of Lenin's organized party was thus extended to the soviets and also to the rest of the state apparatus formed after 1917. The result was an extreme form of hegemonistic integration of a political entity and the first example of the Marxist-Leninist party-state, the Soviet Union.

Seeing the ideology from its aspect of a part in relation to a whole helps reveal the dynamic relation between Marxism-Leninism and the party-state's rule of Russia and a multinational empire through its various phases from Lenin to Brezhnev. It also provides a vantage point for discerning factors that increase or decrease the potential for systemic change in today's USSR.

Elements of Rule

In examining any system of rule we can usually distinguish three generic elements. The stability of any system of rule rests on at least a rough harmony between these elements. The *first* is what may be called the political religion or, alternately, the public orthodoxy of the system. It provides the basis for consensus among its members, at least of those who participate in one way or another in the exercise of authority. It may be a totalist ideology as in the Soviet case or be simply a set of publicly recognized principles or beliefs about the ultimate basis and justification of political association as, say, in the American case.

The *second* element consists of a principle or notion of authoritative rulership or leadership that determines *who,* broadly speaking, shall rule or command and how that rule or command shall be exercised. The principle or notion of rule confers legitimacy to those holding power.

The *third* element is the definition of the collective or communal identity of those subject to the ruling power and in whose name it is exercised.

The court philosopher and chief minister of Alexander III, Pobedonostsev, expressed the above triad of elements with respect to the czardom in his famous formula of Orthodoxy, Autocracy, and Nationality (*Pravoslaviye, Samoderzhavie,* and *Narodnost*). The triad of the Soviet party-state, at least in its original formulation, might be phrased as follows: Marxism-Leninism, Communist party (*partiinost*), the Workers. The American triad is perhaps these three: Self-evident Truths, Constitution, "We, the People."

It seems fairly obvious that any significant change within any one of these three basic elements will affect the other two in one way or another. Also outside changes that impinge on the sphere in which the element operates can affect the harmony and vitality of the whole. Any such changes, if out of tune with the original harmony of the systemic triad, will put strain on it and, if profound enough, endanger its existence.

The formative, unifying, and system-maintenance function of a political religion (used in the broadest sense or ideology, its counterpart) should not be underestimated in assessing the condition of a political system. It often is not given proper weight, not only because of the great difficulty of its analysis, but also because of the predominance of explanations of politics in terms of material interests, conflict over power, or of what are thought to be realistic-pragmatic factors over and against what are thought to be nebulous ideational factors. Often these preconceptions amount to little more than fashionable intellectual prejudices where the truth in fact lies in a subtle, intricate, and often paradoxical dynamic among all such factors.

It might be worth recalling in this connection that that most

hard-eyed realist of all political theory, Machiavelli, placed the
founders of state religions (not far removed from what we call
political ideology today) in rank and significance above even
the power-political builders of great states. For Machiavelli, a
state religion is the indispensable basis for establishing lasting
political institutions. If he had been able to view the
contemporary world, he would rank Marx before Lenin and
Lenin before Stalin in the establishment of the Soviet party-
state. Marxists have learned not a few of their lessons from
Machiavelli. Lenin was true to his teaching when he said in
What Is To Be Done?—another very realistic look at method in
politics—that "without revolutionary theory there is no
revolutionary movement."[1] The corollary of this thesis of
course is that without Marxist-Leninist ideology there would
be no Soviet party-state. However, for Machiavelli it is crucial
for the founders of a state religion to persuade men that it is not
something they contrived or imposed but that it was
communicated to or uncovered for them by higher powers.
This would be as true of Lenin and his Marxist ideology as it
was for Numa Pompilius, the founder of the oracular religion
of the Roman republic. Machiavelli further says it is essential
that rulers, even if they doubted or disbelieved their own
political religion (which many of his exemplars in fact do),
must yet be perfect deceivers, neither betraying in word or deed
any such doubts. Their claim to rule or legitimacy, he argued,
must rest on a superhuman or divine authority because men
will not trust a group of other mere men (or a man) as their
rulers or accept their command *unless* they are persuaded that
the rulers are in touch or in tune with a reliable and sovereign
power outside themselves.

In Machiavellian terms, then, Khrushchev's attack on Stalin
was a profound breach of the rules for preserving the Marxist-
Leninist ideology in the territories of the Russian empire. The
contemporary potential for major internal change of the Soviet
system finds one of its major sources in the iconoclasm
performed by Khrushchev. The Brezhnev regime has striven to

contain and reduce that potential as one of its principal aims.

However, Khrushchev's iconoclasm simply revealed an original defect in Marxist-Leninist ideology—its explicit rejection of any source of authority or legitimacy for political leadership that in some manner transcends the human sphere. Lenin, of course, sensed no weakness here but only a strength. However, the presence of the defect has been strikingly evidenced in not just Soviet but in general Communist political practice. It is revealed in the prevalence of leader cults in the Communist world—first in the posthumous deification of Lenin, then in the cults of Stalin and Mao and all their lesser imitations from Ho Chi Minh to Castro. The rejection in Marxism-Leninism of transcendent grounds for legitimacy has necessitated in practice the projection of godlike leaders who make no mistakes and who have in their own genius the power to guide humanity into the future. The ideology's substitution of an impersonal "History" for a divine or higher source of authority has been insufficient except perhaps for a small intellectual circle in Marxist-Leninist elites. Hence Khrushchev's breaking of the Stalin link of the chain of the leader cults is of greater gravity for the Soviet system than in other systems where authority rests on other grounds. Brezhnev, and Mao even earlier, understood the destructive potential of Khrushchev's actions. Khrushchev's iconoclasm touched the hidden predicament in the foundations of the Soviet party-state itself. The issue of leadership legitimacy inevitably pointed to the basic question of the legitimacy of the party-state itself.

In founding the Soviet party-state, Lenin had no intention of founding a "true" state or political community in the usual sense. In his view the Soviet state was supposed to be a transitory, not a permanent, entity. His narrow and reductionist conception of the state as merely the coercive apparatus of a ruling class—in this case the party leadership as the proxy of the proletariat—and of "politics" as merely the veil of "class struggle," both of which are scheduled for liquidation, profoundly affected the establishment of the Soviet Union as a system of rule. The resulting hybrid party-state is a system, "a structure of power," but in some basic sense not a normal or true state. The vast and historically unprecedented magnification of the coercive and propaganda agencies that have characterized the system are in themselves evidence of this. Lenin and his successors clearly conceived the party-state as dualistic. However, the state was to be the party's double-edged sword. It must use one cutting edge for revolutionary change and yet protect itself from the other edge; the party must always be wary of the state, or elements within the state, turning against the party.

From the outset Lenin designed the Soviet party-state with a view to its intended function as an agency of revolution at home and abroad. It was to be an autonomous entity with respect to the ruling ideas and influences of the modern world. It was to master that great modern trinity of democracy, industrialism, and, above all, nationalism. Much of Soviet history, in fact, has been a history of the rulers' struggles to harness and contain these nether powers. They have veiled totalitarian dictatorship behind an elaborate, but powerless, superstructure of representative institutions. They have chained the forces of industrialism to the political aims of the party-state, seeking to prevent "economics" from gaining sway over "politics" and "ideology." Their most complicated and paradoxical self-appointed task has been the attempt to substitute the "class" notion of solidarity, i.e., "proletarian internationalism," for national consciousness, while at the same time seeking to siphon off indigenous patriotism into a new reservoir of "Soviet patriotism" representing no specific nationality.

It is with respect to this third element of our triad—the question of the collective or communal identity of those who are ruled—that the predicament of the Soviet party-state and its ruling ideology is perhaps at its sharpest. The party institution rests its claim to leadership on its role as an agent of history. It purports to lead not a nation or a people but a class, the proletariat, which in turn serves a future collectivized and yet unseen humanity. The Soviet state rules a "Soviet" people, not a nation in any historical sense but an ideologically-defined entity. For the Soviet party-state to rely on the historical Russian nation in principle and publicly rather than tacitly and obliquely must defeat the expressed purposes of Marxism-Leninism. Yet such a reliance is the precondition for winning genuine national and popular legitimacy in the Russian heartland of the multinational empire it rules.

The weakness of the Soviet party-state in the latter regard was fully revealed in its crisis of survival in World War II. The Stalin regime was carried to safety in that war on a tide of *Russian* patriotism. Neither Communist ideology or its bearer, the party, neither the cult of the leader, nor the apparatus of propaganda and of terror was enough to insure the party-state's survival under the Nazi onslaught. Stalin found himself under another non-Marxian historical necessity. He was compelled to draw on the elemental force of traditional Russian patriotism and even its religious twin, Russian Orthodoxy.

Both the Khrushchev and Brezhnev regimes, in different ways and in turn, have sought to repair the weakness of the party-state's foundation. Both have sought a way of closing the fissure between the party dictatorship and the third element of our triad—in this case primarily the Russian nation and only secondarily to the other nations in territories under Soviet rule.

The Khrushchev Regime

While both leaders aimed above all at preserving the hegemony of the Marxist-Leninist party, Khrushchev tried to build a bridge to the people through his own peculiar brand of revivalist and populist Marxism. It was no accident that Molotov called him a *narodnik*, or populist. His attack on Stalin was, in effect, his promise of an end to the massive coercion and deprivation the party-state under Stalin had perpetrated on its subjects. Simultaneously, Khrushchev began effecting revisions in the first element of our triad—the ideology. All his revisions of Marxist-Leninist doctrine reinforced his attempt to create a stronger base in popular support for the regime. Already his doctrinal revisions at the Twentieth Party Congress in 1956 dampened the dogmas on the inevitability of world wars and violent revolution—dogmas unlikely to win much approval among ordinary Russians in particular. Rather he spoke of the progress of socialist development toward the promised land of communism inside the USSR. He thus began a relative de-emphasis on the function of the Soviet party-state as a *transnational* instrument of a world revolution and an increasing focus on a *national* purpose within the territories of its dominion. His new party program at the twenty-second congress pictured the long-dormant end goals of Marxism-Leninism as now within reach—namely, the withering of the coercive state apparatus and the advent of the first stage of a Communist society of material abundance. He introduced the novel notion of a party and a state of "the whole people." In classical Marxism neither a party nor a state, even a proletarian state, can be instruments of a whole people but only of a class. Yet despite his pragmatism in such matters, Khrushchev was, nonetheless, moved by strong ideological convictions. His attempt to build a new popular base of strength for the party-state through a broad, political relaxation did *not*, notably, include either tolerance of nationalism or religion. His party program boldly asserted the ideological aim of a future "merger" of nationalities in the USSR, and in his own policy he intensified the persecution of Russian Orthodoxy and sectarian Christianity in the USSR.

Khrushchev also sought to change the character of the rulership, the second element of our systemic triad. He sought to build a new basis for the party's preeminence in the party-state structure, again especially with respect to its functions *inside* the country. He came close in his reforms to making the party institution over into a substitute for a normal state. He de-emphasized its ideological purposes and focused on its mundane functions in domestic life. He abolished the "territorial" party apparatus by dividing it into agricultural and industrial branches. He concurrently sought to reduce the role of the traditional Stalinist state structure by trying to dismantle the centralized ministerial bureaucracy, to localize economic management, and to reduce the role of the coercive agencies of the secret police and the military in Soviet politics. Khrushchev specifically sought to put economics over politics in the party's thinking and base the party apparatus on a "production" principle as he termed it rather than ideology. In essence, he aimed at transforming the dualistic Stalinist-Leninist party-state into a party remolded into a unitary and normalized governing institution fully engaged in the temporal affairs of society.

Against this background Khrushchev's own abortive efforts to carve out a formal office of executive leadership—i.e., to establish a titled chairmanship for himself in the party Presidium—suggests a motive beyond his immediate personal ambition to insure his primacy in the leadership. He obviously envied the ability of the American president to exercise executive leadership with significant constitutional protection from coup d'etat from within the rulership. In fact his own undermining of the leader cult called for the cult's replacement by more ordinary notions of leadership. His proposal at the twenty-second congress for institution of regular rotation of leaders in office—as unlikely to be realized as it was—nonetheless was an attempt to give legitimacy to leadership arrangements. The leader cult has, in fact, been the extraordinary means employed to assure hierarchic and hegemonistic command in collective Communist rulerships peculiarly vulnerable to self-destructive factionalism. Khrushchev sought a way out of the dilemma and in his last years even began speaking of a leader's accountability for his actions before those he ruled—a rather unfamiliar theme in the usual rhetoric of Communist leadership. The tradition of the leader cult rather speaks of the followers' debt to the leader's reputed genius and of the complete allegiance they owe him.

When we review Khrushchev's incumbency, we see that he aimed at important changes in each of the three elements of the systemic triad we have chosen for our analysis—namely, he sought to effect changes in the political religion or ideology, in the notion of the ruling authority, and finally in the identity of the community over which rule is exercised (a whole people rather than a class). The revisions Khrushchev attempted, Solzhenitsyn has rightly said, fell just short of going over the brink of fundamental change in the Soviet system. It is not strange then that Brezhnev's restorationist regime saw in Khrushchev's reforms a dangerous deformation of the party-state structure and a menace to its political-ideological rationale.

The Brezhnev Regime

The Brezhnev-led Politburo made the undoing of Khrushchev's works its first order of business. The pressure from within the ruling group against Khrushchev's reforms had already gained headway well before his actual downfall. This basically negative tendency, however, also destroyed the sense of inward movement and change Khrushchev's dynamism had communicated to the regime and the country at large. The result was a kind of political and psychological state of suspense over a period of years—let us say from late 1962 to perhaps as late as 1970. It is into this political-ideological dry-bed that the stream of specifically *Russian* (not *Soviet*) patriotism begins to surface. A reviving Russian national consciousness, welling from below, has been a visible feature of Soviet life since at least the mid-sixties. The irony of this development is underscored by the strenuous effort of the rulership to fire enthusiasm among youth for revolutionary traditions and to sharpen their ideological consciousness. Instead, peculiarly Russian traditions and sentiments caught hold of their imagination.

Brezhnev, however, has exploited the revived patriotic energy, trying to make it a means of shoring up the party-state rather than letting it become a direct danger. His first notable move in this regard was his rehabilitation of Stalin's reputation as the leader who led the country to victory in World War II. His obvious intention was to restore Stalin as leader of the party-state as the essential historical link between the party-state and the Russian *patria*—a link Khrushchev had strived to sever once and for all.

At the same time the Brezhnev regime substituted a staid and stale Leninist-Stalinist orthodoxy for Khrushchev's anti-Stalinist and optimistic Marxian populism. Specifically rejected was Khrushchev's visionary attempt to place Marxist end goals into a specific programmatic timetable. Instead, the regime returned to reliance on standard Leninist formulas. It renewed emphasis on the thesis that a protracted revolutionary process in the outside world must give the basic shape to internal policy—in brief, there can be no "goulash" Communism around the corner. In fact this ideological marking time in part accounts for the Brezhnev leadership's seeking to draw surreptitiously on renewed patriotic energies and to satisfy through a concessionary policy the increased material expectations that Khrushchev's program had aroused inside the country.

Brezhnev's treatment of the defects in the foundations of the party-state has focused on preservation and stabilization—the latter term aptly used by Roy Medvedev to describe the policy of the present leadership.[2] Rather than attempt basic architectural alterations, Brezhnev has labored to preserve the basic structure of the party-state and the traditional relationship between its principal parts—the party, the secret police, the military, and the military-industrial establishment. He has reasserted the Stalinist tradition of rulership arrangements in restoring the titles of Politburo to the ruling oligarchy and general secretary to himself as the chief executor of party policy. The leadership's political-ideological supremacy over and autonomy within the party-state are symbolized in the shift back to the old titles. Crucial to maintaining the vitality of this composite of parts, in the Brezhnevian view, is the steady, if gradual, projection of the power and influence of the party-state into the outside world. From the outset he directed the broad and massive buildup of military strength that has made itself so visible to the world at large. Brezhnev seems to entertain no doubts that the minions of the party-state must be provided with a global mission as a means of sustaining a unity of sorts among them. However, what we are now seeing is not simply the revolutionary messianism of either the Leninist or even the Stalinist regime. Rather, Brezhnev has tried to harness the imperial patriotism of the Russian military and adminis-trative service classes of the Soviet state to the political-ideological expansionism of the Communist elite. He has sought to do this mainly by playing on the cult of the might (*moguchestvo*) of the state. Punctuating his self-identification with this theme of his incumbency, he assumed, after the Twenty-fifth Party Congress, the rank of marshal of the Soviet Union and publicly confirmed his position as head of the State Defense Committee (similar to Stalin's position in World War II).

The increased outward thrust of the Soviet state in foreign affairs over the past decade expresses not only the primary imperative of Marxist-Leninist dogma, but also a kind of high-risk compensation for Russian national consciousness and culture repressed by domestic ideocracy. This broad strategy is likely to prosper as long as outside success comes easily and no serious setbacks occur. Its two elements—Leninist interna-tionalism and imperial patriotism—can be made to overlap, as Brezhnev has done with some degree of skill. Yet they are not the same, and at base and in inspiration they are profoundly at odds. As Stalin so well understood, patriotic and nationalistic trends can erode the ideological bases of party rule. However, it is precisely the seeming, if not actual, compatibility between the party-state's demand for total obedience from its subjects and a traditional allegiance to the Russian imperium that has made linking them together tempting to Brezhnev. Yet the danger of an alternative to party leadership arising out of the military and nationalistically-oriented elements in the administrative elite is ever present in the background of Soviet politics. The new patriotic energies, of course, may be successfully sublimated by the party-state, though not without affecting that entity's own character and behavior. However, it is at least a question whether the two disparate elements of Marxism-Leninism and Russian national consciousness can be made to adhere for long without the presence of a supreme dictatorial power in a single hand.

The hybrid regime of Brezhnev also depends for its continued existence on preserving its relative ideological isolation from outside influences. The revisionist strains of Communism that erupted in Czechoslovakia in 1968 and present-day Eurocommunism, if permitted to take seed in the Soviet party-state, would endanger the Brezhnev hybrid.

Brezhnev's pragmatic-orthodox restoration does resemble to some degree a dialectical outcome of a movement from Stalin's Gulag-based monolith through Khrushchev's de-Stalinizing reformist regime. The Stalin thesis is countered by the Khrushchev negation and then by Brezhnev's negation of the negation. Yet that result may be more an unstable blend than a solid synthesis. A sign that the latter may be closer to the case is evident in the Brezhnev Politburo's extreme delay in bringing a cadre of younger leaders into its topmost ranks. As a result the Politburo has become a collective gerontocracy. Not simply the usual inherent difficulty facing a prime leader in safely selecting a political heir, here is an entire incumbent leadership seemingly unable or unwilling to prepare for the change in political generations. It scarcely testifies to the present rulership's confidence in the inherent strength of the Politburo as an *institution* of rule. This peculiar reluctance of the ruling group as a whole to open the door to the future may register a deep unease over systemic stability—the immediate causes of which are not fully visible to us.

While the entrenchment of the Soviet party rulership in terms of sheer coercive and organizational *power* is indeed great, the firmness of its *authority* is not self-evident. Its survival in revolution, war, crises, and leadership changes since Stalin's death is impressive; but stability is not necessarily sturdiness, nor are imposing outworks identical with inward strength. The contemporary leadership itself since Stalin's death betrays a persisting fear that a false move may begin the unraveling of the system. In his memoirs Khrushchev vividly recalls the leaders' forebodings in the period after Stalin's death of disintegration setting in.[3] After his fall his successors registered their anxiety over the ideological and political indiscipline that Khrushchev's anti-Stalinism introduced into Soviet society. Currently their fears of the hidden potentialities in the small human rights movement in the USSR and Eastern Europe are shown in a vacillating policy of suppression and a manifest lack of confidence in their own strength to tolerate any nonrevolutionary and law-abiding dissent within the system. These are signs that the rulership itself is not sure that its authority (based on Marxist-Leninist ideology), as distinct from its power, runs deep. Authority, when present, is evidenced by the free and willing attachment of the ruled to rulership and the system it directs. Obedience exacted primarily by reliance on coercive power and the threat of its use is the result of power rather than authority. The Soviet rulership in its search for authority beyond its power has had to seek it indirectly and precariously from other sources of legitimation—Khrushchev by championing popular welfare even over revolution and Brezhnev by a disguised appeal to the Russian sense of nationhood. Khrushchev's de-Stalinizing zeal, which was tied to his welfare policy line, came close to precipitating major change inside the party-state itself before the Brezhnev coalition applied the brakes. The reaction of that coalition to a genuine liberalizing party-state in Czechoslovakia in 1968 arose fundamentally out of its concern that the Czech experiment, if allowed to prosper, would have activated the potentialities for basic internal change not only in the national Communist party-states of Eastern Europe but in the USSR itself.

That potentiality in the USSR was made manifest first in the birth of the anti-Stalinist literary movement under Khrushchev. It grew into the spontaneous and autonomous literary, and now embryonic, public culture known as the Democratic Movement. A broad and variegated literature of that movement has emerged since the mid-sixties under the name of *samizdat* (literally, self-publishing). The movement arose wholly within the context of contemporary Soviet society, and its members were all subjects of the regime's sustained effort at total Marxist-Leninist socialization. Within its ranks, however, are figures whose philosophical, literary, and political lineages represent a wide spectrum of modern and traditional schools of thought. Among them can be found Westernizers and Slavophiles,[4] Jews, Christians, socialists, liberals, and some who see themselves as true Marxist-Leninists who reject the Stalinist legacy. Whether Slavophile and Russian patriot (e.g., Solzhenitsyn), Westernizing liberal (e.g., Sakharov), or true Marxist-Leninist (e.g., Roy Medvedev), most of the dissenters share a basic consensus. They agree on the moral necessity for a recovery of the precepts of civility and respect for the individual human personality as a precondition of developing a broad public culture in their country. In combating the regime's harassment and persecution, they have exploited to the hilt the trappings of the rule of law and constitutional rights of the Soviet constitution—virtually all reject violent revolution as an appropriate means to the above ends. Using the leverage of the Soviet written constitution and the aid of Western public pressures, they have forced the Soviet rulership to wriggle on the horns of its own double standard of operation—lip service to civil law and right but application of extralegal methods in practice.

The movement has breached a critical institution of the total party-state—i.e., the latter's complete monopoly over public expression and the formative agencies of public opinion. Obviously the movement is at the mercy of the rulership in terms of sheer coercive power, but the Brezhnev Politburo has taken its challenge to the sway of the Marxist-Leninist political ideology very seriously. It seeks to prevent the *psychic* change that began in the dissident movement under the inspiration of such imposing figures as Solzhenitsyn and Sakharov from spreading beneath the surface of official Soviet life and affecting the infrastructure of the party-state itself. Ultimately, that change could loosen the grip of the party-state on both Russia and the other nations within the empire.

Conclusion

The problem that has begun to ripen in the Brezhnev years—the problem of authority and legitimacy—has its origins, as has been indicated, in Lenin's founding of the Soviet party-state itself. He had no intention of founding a political society or state as such, or for that matter a political culture in its comprehensive and deeper senses. He did indeed produce a structure of ideocratic power—a "system," if you will—which Stalin magnified. Its basic flaw lies in its demonstrated incapacity to produce or prepare the ground for the flowering of an autonomous or original "culture"—either political, literary, artistic, philosophical, or religious. Genuine developments in these spheres have come forth in spite of and not because of the system.

As the system leaves ever further behind it phases of revolutionary upheaval and transformation, the flaw becomes more obvious and a danger to the rulership. If we use the term *political* in more than a rudimentary or technical sense, the measure of a political culture lies in its capacity to provide the conditions for the birth of culture in its higher and more comprehensive expression. Such an expression is a prime source of long-term vitality for the political system itself. The Soviet system—as a political system only in a minimal sense—

has so far shown only a capacity to reproduce itself. In the past decade or so its principal success has been the reproduction of itself in the form of a kind of postrevolutionary stasis.

However, the dilemma that the Marxist-Leninist ideology poses for the contemporary Soviet rulership is that it calls for "forward movement" and "progress" for its validation. Khrushchev tried to meet that demand through a dynamic internal policy, which, however, gave rise to spontaneous tendencies in Soviet society. The latter, in turn, threatened the ideocratic system of the party-state and raised the spectre of its disintegration. Brezhnev, to avoid this outcome, seeks to validate the rulership through a policy of forward movement in the outside world as well as using the outside world as a deus ex machina for making progress at home. It is a policy trusting more to fortune than to foresight. The paradox of the Soviet system, then, in this last half of the twentieth century might be stated this way: If the system's rulership were to begin to permit the spontaneous growth of a public life and culture, it would at the same time start to destroy itself. If, on the other hand, it seeks to stabilize the party-state in immobility and stifle the cultural energies of the society it rules, it could slowly suffocate itself. This may not express a new truth about the Soviet ideocratic system, but it is a truth that presses more forcefully on that system with the passage of time.

Notes

1. V. I. Lenin, *Selected Works*, vol. 1 (Moscow, 1970), p. 138.
2. See Roy Medvedev's opening essay in "The Twentieth Century" *(Dvadtsati vek)* (London: T.C.D. Publications, 1976).
3. For example, Khrushchev recalls in his memoirs the fears over permitting a thaw in Soviet literature after Stalin's death. Khrushchev says, "We were scared — really scared. We were afraid the thaw might unleash a flood which we wouldn't be able to control and which could drown us. How could it drown us? It could have overflowed the banks of the Soviet riverbed and formed a tidal wave

which would have washed away all the barriers and retaining walls of our society. From the viewpoint of the leadership, this would have been an unfavorable development. We wanted to guide the progress of the thaw so that it would stimulate only those creative forces which would contribute to the strengthening of socialism." See Strobe Talbott, ed. and trans., *Khrushchev Remembers: The Last Testament* (Boston: Little, Brown and Co., 1974), p. 79.

4. These twin terms represent a division among Russian intellectuals reaching into the previous century, the former taking the Western culture and the latter indigenous Russian traditions as the basis for their country's cultural development.

3

The Leading Role of the Party: Is There a Change?

Sidney Ploss

The concept of the Communist party's leading role in society has long been the guiding principle of political organization in the Soviet Union. From Stalin to Brezhnev the legal status of the CPSU (Communist Party of the Soviet Union) as outlined in the USSR constitution has been immutable: "vanguard of the working people" and "leading core of all organizations of the working people, both public and State." Official statements on the party's main functions have not been altered; it is still depicted as unifying the system of government by formulating a single policy and coordinating all administrative bodies for its implementation. "Democratic centralism," the core assumption of which was always "the unconditionally binding nature of the decisions of higher bodies for lower ones," is the durable theory of inner-party management.

Whether Soviet rulers are still interpreting such doctrine in basically the old way is a matter of controversy. Some observers have postulated the existence of new trends in the CPSU that add up to its pragmatic evolution. Breezes, if not winds, of change are allegedly bringing a diffusion of power on the Russian internal scene: the regular apparatus of the party is viewed as losing its predominance over the technical intelligentsia, and dogmatic ideology is believed to be in an advanced stage of decay. The Soviet Union, in other words, is imagined to be progressing in the spirit of Menshevik social-democracy and not Bolshevik-style despotism. Albanian Communists and some American political scientists have been the foremost exponents of this interpretation.

Clearly the Soviet structure is vulnerable to the law of change. The method of government and policymaking procedures were revised after Stalin died in 1953 and Khrushchev was ousted in 1964. Coercion as a means of commanding obedience was reduced in scale with the disgrace of the Stalinist secret police, and the rise of political arrests since Khrushchev has failed to approach the massive dimensions of the Gulag era. The top man has not been so strong following intermittent reassertions of the collective leadership principle but must exercise power more tactfully. As a consequence of these developments, bureaucratic defiance of orders and lobbying in behalf of special interests have grown into major troubles for the Kremlin. A human rights movement of international fame has also begun to emerge in the atmosphere of softened dictatorship.

But it is unwarranted to conclude from the drift away from orthodoxy that the party's leading role is turning into just another shibboleth of Soviet politics. The concept is still given vitality by the direction of much economic/social life from a single center in which party officials are better represented than are professional elements. The party is regarded as the best channel through which to seek additional funds for regional growth and redress of local grievances. Streams of enmity are still poured out against a host of alien ideologies, and a regression of party doctrine toward Stalinist positions has narrowed the margin of maneuver in legitimate public discussion of the nation's affairs.

As always, intrigues go on in ruling councils over functions and funds. These conflicts are important for us insofar as they affect the balance of forces in party leadership and the Soviet global posture, which is dependent on it. Divergent attitudes toward defense appear to have created especially acute problems in the party-army relationship and formulation of Soviet armaments policy. But the dispersal of power at top level and hegemonic outlook of all party leaders can be expected to preclude the onset of far-reaching domestic reform or international conciliation in the near term.

Power and Community

The essential feature of Stalinism was one leader's right to make policy decisions and senior appointments on his own without fear of effective challenge. Stalin gained this unique authority by taking charge of the political police in 1936 and instituting a bloodbath against real or imagined opposition currents in party and society. As autocrat, Stalin ruled through a hierarchy of personal aides, central and regional party secretaries, and police chiefs. The scale of influence was ordinarily weighted against state technical experts, who favored emphasis on professional criteria of efficiency in managing the planned economy. Army leaders, too, were usually mere objects of the dictator's policies. Although Stalin was scornful of the niceties of "inner-party democracy" and destroyed the oldtime feeling of solidarity among Communists, he did nevertheless insure the survival of fundamental Bolshevik tradition. Social spontaneity was curbed; the appeal of Western modes of thought neutralized; and party bosses acted as the governors of Soviet territories.

None of Stalin's heirs would prove to be so mighty and decisive a leader. Khrushchev and Brezhnev in the main had to govern by negotiating with colleagues in the rarefied heights who no longer trembled before the general party secretary and his henchmen. Absence of personal rule may go far to explain the widespread laxity and even contumacy that has afflicted Soviet bureaucracy in recent years. As if taking revenge for their onetime humiliation, the state economic planners are unwilling to comply with party directives that require an unsettling change of their routine practice. The military officers' corps has tended to show a remarkable independence of thought, and regional party staffs have often petitioned for lower production quotas than Moscow set for their areas. Brezhnev would have to address himself openly to the "problem" of failure to carry out the decisions of higher bodies, telling the Twenty-fifth Party Congress that as many as three orders were sometimes needed before action was taken, and he revealed that the Politburo had sent a special letter on the subject to all party branches.[1] The outer world, of course, is more familiar with such recent change in Soviet official conduct as the toleration of some intellectual protest against the persecution of literary/artistic nonconformists and discrimination suffered by ethnic/religious groups. Yet the central party machine is the greatest source of policy initiative and administrative power inside the USSR today.

The Party Rules stipulate that it is the CPSU Central Committee (CC) that "directs the activities of the Party" between its quinquennial congresses. If true, this would mean a rather equitable sharing of power among the diverse bureaucratic formations and a most careful sounding of local/ nationality opinion in view of the wide-gauge composition of the Central Committee. Supreme power, however, clearly rests with the CC CPSU Politburo, which is authorized "to direct the work of the CC between plenary meetings," and Secretariat, which is "to direct current work, chiefly the selection of personnel and the verification of the fulfillment of party decisions." Only 11 Central Committee Plenums were held in the almost five-year period from the twenty-fourth congress (April 1971) to the twenty-fifth congress (February 1976); 215 Politburo meetings and 205 Secretariat meetings were held in the same time frame.[2] Aside from the infrequency of Plenums, the Central Committee cannot be regarded as a deliberative body if only because of its unwieldy size—over 300 full members—and the one- or two-day duration of its sessions. The lack of recent information about how the Central Committee exercises its statutory right of electing Politburo members and about consultations between Plenums gives added reason to deem the Central Committee members a prestige elite responsive to the wishes of a power elite in the Politburo/Secretariat.

Unlike the hundreds of Central Committee members, who are described collectively as "eminent Party and State figures," the Politburo's fifteen full members are exalted as "leaders of the highest Party and State bodies, more eminent and experienced political figures."[3] A majority of them are party workers as distinct from state technical experts, a circumstance that cannot ensure an identity of views on all issues, but may on some which relate to the question of which bureaucracy—party or state—should have primacy. An admission of the persistence of this historical dilemma was the charge of Khrushchev's faction that its rivals in the 1957 Anti-party Group who tended to concentrate on the state bureaucracy "waged a struggle against . . . the directing role of the Party" (*Pravda*, November 12, 1958). Concretely, the late premier's memoirs give an inkling of how the dilemma's resolution impacts on bringing new technology to the public and ultimately raising its living standards:

> It has become the rule in our country for Party organizations virtually to dictate orders to farms and factories. And where do those orders originate? All too often they come from on high, from uninformed central authorities who end up doing more harm than good. . . . In our system, the number one man is always the Party leader. But the Party should play a strictly *political* role, and technical questions should be left to the experts. In this age of increasingly complicated technology, no political leader can keep abreast of the latest developments. As the Americans have shown us, our administrators must be professionals and specialists if we want to catch up.[4]

A more recent reminder of the practical import of the party-state dichotomy was served in *Pravda*'s (December 16, 1976) recollection that Brezhnev as party boss of Kazakhstan in the

1950s fought with "many specialists" who doubted the wisdom of plowing up massifs of virgin soil in that arid region. Thus, the old disposition of many party organizers to put politics ahead of professionalism lingers on, albeit the effect of policy must vary in accord with changing constellations of power within the senior echelons of the regime.

What is constitutionally the highest organ of state authority, the USSR Supreme Soviet, is still a party-controlled rally to symbolize national unity and not an authentic parliamentary forum. The mechanism for party regulation of Supreme Soviet proceedings is disclosed in a work of the USSR Academy's Institute of State and Law:

> All legislative acts in the country are adopted by the USSR Supreme Soviet and, in the intervals between its sessions, by the Supreme Soviet Presidium with their subsequent ratification at the Supreme Soviet session. Naturally, any draft law, or *ukaz*, of great social-political importance for the country is examined beforehand in the CC CPSU, which gives its recommendations. . . . When any draft law which has undergone preliminary discussion is then brought to the USSR Supreme Soviet, the CC CPSU cannot obligate all deputies to accept or reject it. The CC can only obligate the Supreme Soviet's deputies who are Party members, comprising the Party Group in it, which works under the direct leadership of the CC, to uphold at the session the draft law as a whole or amendments and changes. If new proposals arise in the course of discussion, the Party Group takes a unified position in regard to it.[5]

Since about 70 percent of the Supreme Soviet deputies are party members or candidates, no key law is apt to be enacted without the approval of party headquarters. Nor has the party lost its monopoly on the right of legislative initiative. Even in Stalin's day, so-called public organizations had this prerogative: the Soviet Committee for Defense of Peace was said to have inspired the Supreme Soviet's 1951 Law on Defense of Peace. The 1961 Party Program extolled this practice and in 1970 new labor-law guidelines enabled the All-Union Central Council of

Trade Unions to promote legislation. But as a monograph of the CC CPSU Academy of Social Sciences apprises, the party exercises nothing less than "direct leadership" of the trade unions.[6]

As a rule, no effort is made to disguise the Party's mastery of the law-sponsorship process. The initiative for CC CPSU decrees, which have the force of law, is occasionally attributed to the general secretary or departments of the CC CPSU Secretariat; state laws are said to have been recommended by the general secretary, Politburo, or Party Congress. The USSR Council of Ministers, or government cabinet, is sometimes "entrusted" by the CC CPSU to work out the details for its decrees but evidently has some discretionary power. An example of how some joint decrees of party and government originate is given by the party first secretary of Smolensk Oblast, who sent a memo to the CC CPSU requesting more state investment in local agriculture. Brezhnev is said to have routed the memo to appropriate officials with the notation, "I ask you to examine and prepare a draft decree envisaging help to an immemorial Russian oblast that suffered in the war."[7]

The federal party Secretariat still wields much power and influence. Along with the Politburo, it reportedly reviews and makes decisions on current questions of both domestic and foreign policy.[8] The "brigades" of Secretariat departments investigate local state agencies and bring their findings to the secretaries' attention in memos.[9] Assignments to sensitive governmental posts must be cleared at the Secretariat; a text of the party's Academy of Social Sciences devoted to external affairs affirms that while "decisions on the appointment of workers of the foreign-relations organs are taken by the highest bodies of State power and administration, . . . the Party does not stand to the side of this question." "V.I. Lenin," it asserts, "constantly pointed out the duty of central Party bodies to concern themselves with cadres of diplomats. . . . Following Leninist instructions, the Party in practice decides cadre questions, selecting and recommending to appropriate State bodies people who meet the high present-day requirements and are experienced workers."[10] In reality, cronyism and cliquishness are still the major determinants of upward political mobility. An illustrative case is that of CC CPSU secretary for agriculture since 1965, F.D. Kulakov. From 1944-50 he was chief of the Agricultural Department in the offices of the Penza Regional Party Committee. One of the regional committee secretaries from 1945-48 was K.U. Chernenko, who later served under Brezhnev in the CC CP Moldavia and Secretariat of the USSR Supreme Soviet Presidium. Soon after Brezhnev acquired Khrushchev's mantle, Chernenko was named chief of the General Department in the CC CPSU Secretariat, and Kulakov was elevated from a party job in the provinces to headship of the CC CPSU Agricultural Department. At the same time, the CPSU Secretariat has ordered local counterparts to maintain a narrower sphere of personnel assignment (*nomenklatura*) than was once the case, and the extent of party-political control over state job appointments varies from one union republic to another.[11]

The actual locus of decision-making power over party and state concerns evidently fluctuates with the shifting personal fortunes of top leaders. After the Twenty-fifth Party Congress, for example, there was a striking disarray in Soviet media over the relative importance of the Politburo and Secretariat. Some oddly listed the Secretariat before the Politburo while others did the reverse in holding up models of political work style.[12] Authors of major articles in CPSU propaganda journals differed as to whether the Secretariat was involved in the party's direction of foreign policy.[13] This discordance may have reflected a competition for power among various leadership groups, with materials unfavorable to the Politburo indicating a desire to cut state officials like Foreign Minister Gromyko out of the policymaking huddles and concentrate authority in the hands of the most illustrious *apparatchiki* (members of the party apparatus).

Since the party chiefs have monopolized freedom of

discussion about high policy, they insinuate that the country is still surrounded by enemies, making it unsafe to examine the most vital questions in broad daylight. An implicit maxim of ideological encirclement justifies the reaching of key decisions in a small circle behind closed doors, and the workings of the apparatuses for securing conformity. Anti-Soviet forces are identified as internal dissidents and local patriots; East European nationalists and reform Communists; "aggressive imperialistic circles"; world Zionism; and, until the Great Helmsman's demise, Chinese Maoists. The very same linkage of foreign and internal adversaries of the regime that Stalin made for over a quarter century is to be found in guidance that the CC CPSU Higher Party School and Academy of Social Sciences provides to party workers:

> Only revisionists and renegades who have lost all sense of reality can assert that after the events denoting a certain easing of international tension a period has dawned when it will be possible not only to conclude foreign-political, economic and scientific-technical agreements between the lands of capitalism and socialism, but also to establish ideological coexistence, halt the ideological struggle in the sphere of social thought and all spiritual culture.
>
> Reactionary imperialistic circles advertise to the whole world the writings and utterances of A. Solzhenitsyn, A. Sakharov and their ilk which are hostile to socialism and the Soviet people. The actions of these renegades coincide fully with the plans and calculations of sworn enemies of our Homeland and the entire world of socialism who call for a "total coexistence" which requires the lands of socialism to take down their "ideological fortifications."[14]

Caution has become more noticeable in political theorizing, which signals the limits of public dialogue about micro-issues and reflects to some extent the real condition of the Soviet leaders' mind. The USSR is no longer represented as being in a stage of "full-scale building of communism," as claimed by Khrushchev, who thereby raised expectations of less social inequality and steps toward the transfer of executive rights from the state machine to public organizations. Only a phase of "developed" or "mature" socialism is now recognized, which tends to establish a firmer link with the Stalinist past, when advent of the classless and stateless society of full communism was put over the mountains. The overprivileged bureaucratic strata, KGB (State Security Committee), and army could only have welcomed this regression in political theory.

The regime's steady drumbeat of Manichaean propaganda and its subjects' awareness of police muscle in the background have kept very thin the ranks of non-Communists who venture to speak out against what they regard to be social injustice. Kremlin willingness to allow some vocal political dissent on the fringes is explicable in terms of the leaders' courtship of Western public opinion during a period of international détente. If, however, the dissidents' calls for free criticism and social control should cause a stir in the unsophisticated Soviet public, party chiefs are likely to intensify the selective terror they have easily practiced for more than a decade. The world of politics, of course, is full of surprises, and the neo-Marxian school of dissident thought could be a potential future alternative for the CPSU, which has never been entirely purged of the original revolutionary idealism (Trotskiism) and moderate socialist outlook (Bukharinism).

Clashes of Viewpoints

Within the framework of full-blown and modified totalitarianism, there have normally been party intrigues over power and policy. Stalin, in the postwar period, had to arbitrate disputes among his lieutenants over the degree to which industrial managers could be liberated from central party control (Zhdanov versus Malenkov); forms of labor organization inside the collective farms, or kolkhozes (Andreyev versus Khrushchev); and prospects for collaboration with the West (Molotov versus Mikoyan). On all scores, the Georgian allowed the forces of dogmatism to prevail over those of evolution.

After Stalin reformist ideas were circulating in society, and some did penetrate into the highest circles. All of the following critics reported by Koerner and Roeder in their "Russian Notebook" hated "the rigid system of centralized planning, with its fixed targets for everybody, which they regard as the root cause of bureaucratic corruption, poor quality output, and personal insecurity." They agreed that "the failure of agriculture" was "the most vital national problem." Moderates sought "less detailed planning and greater freedom of initiative for both factory and kolkhoz managers; they want a kind of socialist market economy, with fewer 'targets' and 'campaigns' and more incentives." These people wished to preserve the kolkhozes but allow them to produce what they thought they could sell best. Radicals wanted to replace the kolkhoz by "voluntary cooperatives of individual peasants" and the creation of "democratic trade unions and peasant organizations" that could play a major role in deciding economic policy and administering production."[15]

The radical current of opinion was ignored by Stalin's heirs, who were all wedded to a paternalistic outlook on industrial and farm labor. But for more than twenty years, there would be leadership quarrels over the moderate program for economic rationalization and sporadic outbreaks of the postwar controversies. The closed nature of decision-making forums and their domination by party organizational men with a bunker mentality has virtually guaranteed a setback for risk takers in the policy disputes.

Search for proper definition of party role has lurked behind the clashes of viewpoints about industry, agriculture, and defense. In another of the ironic episodes with which Soviet history abounds, Brezhnev, who at first flayed Khrushchevian "subjectivism," came to display no less determined a will to assert the clear predominance of the party machine in economics and strategy. Only after much wrangling, however, did Brezhnev succeed in hurdling opposition to an enlargement of the party apparat's order-giving authority in the countryside and defense ministry. An alliance of neo-Zhdanovist party officials and state technologists seems to be still resisting a Brezhnev-led drive to tighten party control in industry.

Various solutions to the industrial efficiency problem commended themselves to Khrushchev's successors. Premier Kosygin, as foremost representative of the technical intelligentsia, obviously favored more use of money relations, market prices, and the calculation of profits and losses within the context of central planning. Kosygin also stood for minimizing party interference in the direction of varied industrial sectors from Moscow ministries.[16] Brezhnev and Suslov, the senior party secretaries, went on record as foes of genuine economic reform by virtue of their sharp attacks on "narrow practicism" and "technocratic positions."[17] The party head is likely to have concurred with those who went a step further and advocated loss of some ministerial right to regional capitals, where the party staffs were very influential.[18] A third school, exemplified by Party Secretary Kirilenko, seems to have urged a combination of greater accent on the profit motive and an easing of day-to-day party control without harming the central economic agencies.[19] The actual course of policy has wavered from acceptance of elements of Kosygin's "economic" approach to more dependence on the "structural" panacea of Brezhnev/Suslov, but has stopped short of radical revamping of Kosygin's empire. Brezhnev, to be sure, has made a certain tactical concession to the pressure for harnessing the party's energies to less practical tasks in industry, and the business executives have been able to resume their campaign for a new round of limited economic reform.[20] It remains to be seen how much headway can be made toward overcoming the tradition of letting the last word be spoken by party officials, who are (to use Khrushchev's word) "uninformed."

The regime's failure to boost agricultural output despite new investment programs has sparked a number of disputes between diehards in the General Secretariat and revisionist forces. An extraordinary proposal to abolish crop quotas for kolkhozes and introduce the free contracting of products, with prices shaped by supply and demand, brought down a storm of criticism from the Secretariat's Agricultural Department.[21] A *Pravda* article of March 4, 1968, finally put a lid on the discussion about introducing freedom of trade for kolkhozes. Republic Premier and Politburo member Voronov personally approved of trying to break the crusty apathy of the peasants by assigning machinery to small teams, or "links," for long periods of time, with payment to be based on the harvest (*Komsomolskaya Pravda*, May 11, 1969). Brezhnev's refusal to endorse the links on grounds of an implicit threat to the collectivist basis of Soviet farming probably helps to account for the negativism marking relevant proceedings at the Congress of Kolkhozniki in November 1969. The classic party nostrums of farm giantism and administrative pressure were still dear to the heart of Brezhnev, who guided the work of a Politburo commission that drafted the May 28, 1976, decree of the CC CPSU, "Further development of specialization and concentration of agricultural production on the basis of interfarm cooperation and agro-industrial integration" (*Pravda*, June 2, 1976). The USSR Ministry of Agriculture had been scolded at the Twenty-fifth Party Congress for impeding work on a pilot of this scheme, which aims at the pooling of farm resources to pull up weak kolkhozes, merger of agricultural and industrial enterprises, and more peasant investment for production facilities. Agriculture Minister Polyanskiy's removal from the Politburo and journey into diplomatic exile cleared a path for Brezhnev's leveling gambit in the countryside, which was to be executed by kolkhoz councils under party leadership.

Political intimacy between Defense Minister Marshal Grechko and Brezhnev was indicated by Brezhnev's solo flight to army field maneuvers Grechko ran in March 1970 and Grechko's undoubtedly pro-détente speech at the May 1972 Plenum, which approved of a Soviet-American summit meeting in spite of the U.S. president's decision to escalate the Vietnam War. After Grechko was brought into the Politburo at the April 1973 Plenum, however, he openly disagreed with Brezhnev's implication that the USSR should assume a posture of strategic deterrence in order to economize on defense rather than strive for an exceedingly costly war-fighting capability. Brezhnev, in his Havana speech of January 30, 1974, tacitly ruled out the likelihood that the United States would seek a political edge over the Soviet Union by resorting to violence: "It [the capitalist world] has had to recognize the impossibility of solving by military means the historic dispute between capitalism and socialism. . . . War is no longer suitable as an instrument for solving disputes between states, especially between the two social systems. . . . World war with the use of modern means of mass destruction cannot bring advantage to anyone." Civilian officials likewise tended to argue that the superpowers' arsenals made hopeless the resolution of conflicts by a test of arms and that diplomatic compromise was feasible to reduce huge stockpiles of nuclear weapons.[22] In contrast, Grechko and the military theorists averred by indirection that war was still a realistic policy alternative for Western leaders and even stressed outright the value of large numbers of "refined" nuclear weapons.[23] If the premise of the militarists was correct, many up-to-date missiles and MIRVs (multiple independently targeted reentry vehicles) were essential, and a cautious stance at arms limitation talks would be best.

Party leaders evidently felt that it was expedient to accommodate Grechko since on the eve of the Vladivostok summit, where a very high ceiling was placed on missiles and bombers in inconclusive arms limitation talks, *Pravda* (November 13, 1974) carried the frosty words of General Staff Chief Kulikov about war remaining a mere "continuation of policy by other, namely, violent means" and "the presence of strategic nuclear weapons with the constant threat of their use by the imperialistic states." Grechko's sudden death in April 1976 set in train a series of events that appear to have mirrored an attempt to restore unchallengeable party authority over the military. For the first time in almost thirty years, a civilian was named defense minister; Brezhnev was promoted to the rank of marshal, and his glorification as such in Soviet media was almost certainly meant to dramatize the party's intent to strengthen its control over the officers' corps. These unusual developments were accompanied by less insistence on the necessity of bolstering Soviet military power in the statements of party chiefs.[24] Brezhnev in a speech of November 24, 1976, returned to the nuclear-war-is-suicide theme, and Kulikov was shifted to a less important military post (January 8, 1977)—all of which may have signified a reassessment of the vast arms programs that Grechko had demanded.

Ledger of Restraints

In determining whether continuity or change has been the prevalent trend in party role during recent times, one must distinguish between the situation within the political governing class and the regime-people relationship.

At first glance, Khrushchev and Brezhnev would seem to have followed in Stalin's footsteps as supreme ruler of the party and in turn of the state machine and country at large. Each was the leading party secretary, and Khrushchev, like Stalin, since 1941 held the premiership. Both usually were at center stage on the most important political occasions, were never directly contradicted in Soviet media, and had sizeable leader cults (though much less exaggerated than Stalin's). In analysis, however, it looks as if neither Khrushchev nor Brezhnev had the ultimate right to adjudicate all major policy disputes and enable the collective will of the party apparat to prevail at all times. Brezhnev in particular seems to have been vulnerable to pressure from the military and incapable of taming the Moscow industrial experts. Whatever the political support the conservative generals and planners got from top party leaders other than Brezhnev, the party's prestige in the world of Soviet bureaucracy had to suffer as a result of the varied concessions made to special departmental interests.

On the other hand, the decline of the party machine's authority in bureaucratic circles has been relative. It continues to enjoy an advantage at the Politburo, which in line with Leninist tradition makes basic policy and the most senior appointments. The more broadly based Central Committee has been kept in a state of dependency on the Politburo, which can thus afford to pay less attention to regional and non-Russian voices. Governmental operations and staffing remain under the monitorship of the party Secretariat. The inchoate tendency of the Defense Ministry under Grechko to become an independent power center was checked, and for some time the momentum of Kosygin's economic reform was slowed. Nevertheless, a break with the past is most discernible inside the power/prestige elite, which has translated into action its fear of the rise of a new dictator and its longtime craving for stability.

With a few notable exceptions—scientific inquiry and Jewish emigration—continuity asserts itself more clearly in the party's dealings with the population. The leadership's low estimate of the people's socialist maturity can account for the tight leash still kept on the parliamentary and mass organizations. What most Soviet citizens think of their rulers' authoritarian habits can hardly be ascertained, but few are likely to have taken at face value the talk of Khrushchev and Brezhnev about the necessity of making bureaucracy less secretive and more responsible by widening the scope of elections for state posts. Decades of reality indicate that if *glasnost* (making things public) and *vybornost* (the principle of election) are given wider application it will be done with party guardianship as an antidote to local corruption and not permitted to verge on anarchy. As far as one can tell, the multitude gives little thought to the prospects for democratization that are of concern to the small band of intellectual dissenters. The regime, however, may recognize an optimal limit to this not wholly unwelcome mass apathy and cynicism. A reason for the comparative stability of party leadership after Khrushchev may have been an awareness in ruling quarters that too-frequent purges and denunciations of leading figures could serve to undermine popular confidence in government, which in turn might require a steep rise of police coercion. In other words, the incipient crisis of governmental confidence below, which was most visible in the Khrushchev era, acts as a restraint on violent disruption of the unstable equilibrium above.

The internal processes are relatable to conciliatory and hardline thrusts in Soviet foreign policy. Party favoritism of command over market impulses to drive the economy forward is a source of productivity lag the regime hopes to rectify by return to the Leninist stratagem of obtaining financial and technical assistance from the capitalist world. But the primacy of domestic controls has been a stumbling block to improving relations with the top Atlantic powers because the Brezhnev leadership refuses to abandon its restrictive emigration policy for the sake of gaining trade and credit benefits from the United States. The ebb and flow of influence among Soviet bureaucratic heads does something to explain radicalizing tendencies in the conduct of détente. Brezhnev may have wished to brighten the Soviet party apparat's tarnished image of history maker by granting a rare audience in 1975 to the CPSU ideologist Zarodov, who was then urging a line of revolutionary elitism upon West European Communists. The more self-confident Soviet army commanders might have promoted the subsequent escalation of Moscow's involvement in the Angolan civil war. Considerations of domestic politics have also influenced the Kremlin's relations with Warsaw Pact members. A probable reason for the 1968 invasion of Czechoslovakia was to obviate the danger of reform Communist ideas filtering into the USSR, and a stronger CPSU leader than Brezhnev might have resisted a bit longer the demands for intervention that came from a number of sources.

The political belief system of Marxism-Leninism helped to shape the climate of opinion in which the USSR became a suspicious and heavily armed police state with expansionist ambitions. Leninist ideology offered a rationale for establishing and preserving Bolshevik single-party rule in Russia. It instructed that aggressive war is an inherent behavioral trait of Western states. Stalin's creative enrichment of Lenin's teaching laid a "scientific" basis for satisfying a thirst for absolute power over social interests at home and desire for projecting the apparat's influence abroad. Under Khrushchev the most terrifying aspects of this orthodoxy—the fatal inevitability of world war and constantly rising subversion inside the Soviet Union—were discarded. But enough of the corpus of doctrine would survive to raise an important psychological obstacle to the creation of an atmosphere of trust in Moscow's dealings with the outside world and the Soviet citizenry. Only a new autocrat of statesmanlike character would be able to hurdle that barrier, and he has yet to appear over the horizon of Russian politics. In the meantime, piecemeal reform of archaic domestic practices and adherence to a policy of selective co-existence between world power blocs is the most that can reasonably be anticipated from essentially insecure and frequently divided Soviet oligarchs.

Notes

1. Brezhnev's report to the Twenty-fifth Party Congress in *Pravda*, February 25, 1976.

2. Ibid.

3. *Partiynoye Stroitelstvo. Uchebnoye Posobiye. Izd. 2-e, dop.* (Moscow: Politizdat, 1971), pp. 149 and 154.

4. Strobe Talbott, ed. and trans., *Khrushchev Remembers: The Last Testament* (Boston: Little, Brown and Co., 1974), pp. 136, 137-38.

5. *Politicheskaya Organizatsiya Sovetskogo Obshchestva* (Moscow: Nauka, 1967), p. 396.

6. *Politicheskaya Organizatsiya i Upravleniye Obshchestvom pri Sotsializme* (Moscow: Mysl, 1975), p. 123.

7. I. Ye. Klimenko, in *Oktyabr*, no. 7, 1976.

8. *Pravda Vostoka*, December 5, 1975 (N.D. Khudayberdyyev);

Pravda, February 29, 1976 (P.P. Grishkyavichus); and *Problemy Mira i Sotsializma,* no. 8, 1976, pp. 21-27 (K. Chernenko).

9. On the role of Secretariat departments, see *Bakinskiy Rabochiy,* December 18, 1975 (G. A. Aliyev), and June 26, 1976 (CCCP Azerbaijan Decree).

10. *Mezhdunarodnaya Politika KPSS i Vneshniye Funktsii Sovetskogo Gosudarstva* (Moscow: Mysl, 1976), pp. 131-32.

11. *Voprosy Raboty KPSS s Kadrami na Sovremennom Etape* (Moscow: 1976), pp. 173-74.

12. Pro-Secretariat statements are in *Zarya Vostoka,* March 18, 1976 (Ya. I. Kabkov); *Pravda,* March 27, 1976 (A. Viktorov); *Sovetskaya Kirgiziya,* October 27, 1976 (T.U. Usubaliyev); and *Sovetskaya Belorussiya,* December 10, 1976 (V. Zhukov). The Politburo is given prominence over the Secretariat in analogous materials in *Leningradskaya Pravda,* March 17, 1976 (G.V. Romanov); *Partiynaya Zhizn,* no. 12, 1976 (V. Stepanov); and *Pravda,* December 18, 1976 (P. Fedoseyev and Ye. Zhukov).

13. See A.I. Stepanov, who ignores the Secretariat, in *Voprosy Istorii KPSS,* no. 12 (signed to press November 26), 1976, and V. Brovikov, who cites it, in *Agitator,* no. 24 (signed to press December 6), 1976.

14. *Voprosy Vnutripartiynoy Zhizni i Rukovodyashchey Deyatelnosti KPSS na Sovremennom Etape* (Moscow: Mysl, 1974), pp. 30-31.

15. Heinrich Koerner and Bernhard Roeder (repatriated Germans formerly in Vorkuta forced labor camp), "Russian Notebook: 'Silent Pressures' from Below," quoted in *The Observer* (London), June 24, 1956.

16. A.N. Kosygin, *Izbrannye Rechi i Stati* (Moscow: Politizdat, 1974), passim.

17. *Pravda,* December 22, 1971, and L.I. Brezhnev, *Voprosy Agrarnoy Politiki KPSS i Osvoyeniye Tselinnykh Zemel Kazakhstana (Rechi i Doklady)* (Moscow: Politizdat, 1974), pp. 352-53.

18. A. Yemelyanov, *Pravda,* July 25, 1974.

19. A.P. Kirilenko, *Izbrannye Rechi i Stati* (Moscow: Politizdat, 1976), passim.

20. Illuminating material on the party and industry is in *Pravda,* May 18, 1976 (Ye. Kachalovskiy's attack on "unjustified harassment of meritorious and experienced business executives"); *Pravda,* June 23, 1976 (Ya. P. Ryabov's scoring of a party secretary who "did not listen to specialists, ordered people about"); *Pravda,* July 4, 5, and 6, 1976 (Minister K.N. Rudnev for "expanding the financial autonomy

of ministries"); and *Pravda*'s editorial of July 29, 1976 (approving of the Rudnev experiment).

21. G. Lisichkin in *Novyy Mir,* no. 9, 1965, and no. 2, 1967; *Selskaya Zhizn,* September 22, November 29, December 8, 17, and 21, 1966.

22. G.A. Arbatov, *Problems of Peace and Socialism,* no. 2, 1974, pp. 41-47; V.G. Dolgin, *Voprosy Filosofii,* no. 1, 1974, p. 62; and A. Ye. Bovin, *New Times,* no. 30, 1973, p. 19, and *Molodoy Kommunist,* no. 4, 1974, pp. 26-27.

23. Col. Sidelnikov, *Krasnaya Zvezda,* August 14, 1973; Lt. Gen. Lototskiy, *Voyenno-Istoricheskiy Zhurnal,* no. 9, 1973, pp. 4-5 and 7; Col. Rybkin, *Kommunist Vooruzhennykh Sil,* no. 20, 1973, pp. 1126-27; Rear Admiral Shelyag, *Krasnaya Zvezda,* February 7, 1974; and Grechko, *Kommunist,* no. 3, 1974, p. 15.

24. Of special interest are the less truculent formulas about defense in Ustinov's Order for VE Day (*Pravda,* May 9, 1976) and the revisions of Kirilenko's past statements in his *Izbrannye Rechi i Stati,* approved for publication on August 17, 1976.

4

Imperatives of Economic Reform and Communist Political Systems

John P. Hardt

Improving economic performance in the course of the current Soviet Tenth Five Year Plan and the related plans of the countries of the Council for Mutual Economic Assistance (CMEA) is a matter of dominant concern to the leadership. Arresting the slowdown in economic growth and improving the quality of performance are central features of all past five year plans as discussed at their respective Party Congresses. Several means have been suggested in the form of policy choices to bring about improved economic performance: (1) a shift in resource allocation to more growth-generating civilian sectors, away from defense claimants; (2) increased imports of Western technology, especially emphasizing imported plants and equipment for new industrial facilities, agricultural equipment, service-tourist facilities, and transportation equipment; (3) economic reforms to the traditional system of planning and management. Some suggest that international trade might be used as a substitute for either changes in resource allocation policy or economic reform. Elsewhere I have suggested that increased trade with the West may require changes in resource allocation instead of reducing resource policy pressure, i.e., the resource-demanding impact of Western imports might be greater than their resource-releasing function.[1] In this discussion I would like to suggest that increased Western imports, in order to have their desired full effects in increased productivity,

may make selective economic reforms imperative. The pressure
for trade is likely to influence important elements of the
traditional political system of party control as well. Although
the aggregate and short-term effect of this complimentary
pressure on increased trade and reform may be very modest and
the changes in the political system specific to strictly limited
and defined areas, the impact or "ripple effect" of change may
be greater, even in the short run, than the direct effect short-term
change may suggest. In order to illustrate this line of reasoning,
I shall concentrate on the Soviet economy, with only passing
reference to East European experience, and make the following
points:

1. The strategy of improvement in key economic sectors in
recent Soviet plans requires *active* systems of transfer,
absorption, adaption, and diffusion of technology in order to
meet perceived needs.

2. Active systems of technology transfer often require new
institutional forms for accommodating systematic changes.
The use of production associations (*ob'edineniia*), more direct
central party involvement, and more direct access to Western
markets involves a withdrawal of preferred sectors from the
traditional economic structures or an insulation of the
preferred units from the normal administrative process with
specific prerogatives.

3. Changing of party regulations within a preferred
externally related economic sector—a foreign trade sector—
may be no more disruptive to party discipline (*partiinost'*) or
corrosive to the principles of party purity than special
prerogatives to military and military-industrial organizations.
The analogy of an organ transplant to the Soviet body politic,
representing not only infusions of Western plants and
equipment, but also Western systems of management and
incentives, may make an anatomical metaphor relevant. The
pathology or systemic response to modest introductions of a
foreign system may have broader, perhaps, irreversible effects
on the political nature of the system of control while providing

a hospitable climate for economic performance.

Thus we might ask: Is the modest intervention of foreign systems or technological organisms likely to cause a broadening adjustment or reaction in the system as a whole? Can the Soviet political system accommodate and insulate a Western-type economic enclave in its midst? Similarly, are the Hungarian, Polish, and other East European political systems accommodating or insulating Western-type enterprises within their economic structures? Will the transplanting of foreign technological and management organisms require or stimulate a change in the pathology of the systems?

Key Sector Strategy

The Soviet automobile industry was the centerpiece of Western technology transfer during the Eighth and Ninth Five Year Plans as it had been in the first. The decision to bring in Italian engineers and make the Soviet version of the Fiat, the Zhiguli, the standard for passenger car output was a key decision made soon after Khrushchev's removal from power.[2] The decision to develop a new truck plant on the Kama River in the Urals was likewise a step in implementing a progressive economic policy of selective interdependence. With the Ninth Five Year Plan also came a policy of reliance on Western technology for development of oil and gas, chemicals, computer products and usage, and agribusiness. Areas of specific need such as telecommunications, involving an improved telephone system; airport safety, involving radar and related equipment; earth moving equipment for the Baikal-Amur railroad; and containerization for cargo transport all received technological attention.

These sectors of the Soviet economy appear to have adopted a Western technology strategy in the Tenth Five Year Plan (1976-80):

1. Automotive production, including passenger cars and

trucks. The Fiat plant at Tol'yatti and the Kama truck plant in the Urals are still the major projects.

2. Hydrocarbon (oil and gas) output and transmission. Onshore oil and gas is being produced in West Siberia, and offshore resources are being developed off Sakhalin Island and in the Caspian Sea. Tyumen provinces projects include development of natural gas fields referred to as "North Star."

3. Metal processing using direct reduction processes and other major Western technological advancements. A major project at Kursk is the leading current development.

4. Chemical processes ranging from fertilizer output to plastics and petrochemicals. The Kuibyshev fertilizer plants in Volga Valley are among the major undertakings.

5. Computer-assisted systems for a variety of industries, economic analysis, and planning institutions. The large IBM and Control Data systems for *Intourist*, the Kama truck plant, and other facilities are characteristic.

6. Agribusiness technology to provide infrastructure and efficient plant for quality food output, including meat. The importation of feed grain is supplementary to technological change.

7. Tourist facilities. Hotel space, transport facilities, and entire tourist absorption facility for 1980 Summer Olympics and thereafter are being put into place on a priority schedule.[3]

Active System Technology Transfer

Although the Soviet economic sectors stressing Western technology transfer have much to gain as measured by the gap between their levels of technology and those of the Western developed economies, skepticism has been expressed about their ability to utilize the technology effectively.[4] Recent experience fortifies the view that the civilian Soviet economic sectors have difficulty absorbing, adapting, and diffusing the new technology. Moreover, as many of the sectors using Western technology are undergoing dynamic change, including innovation, it is important for them to keep up once they have caught up. Based on studies of technology transfer, a recent Department of Defense study concluded that "active" transfers were necessary to provide effective transplant. Such mechanisms, according to this study, have the following general characteristics:

> "Active" relationships involve frequent and specific communications between donor and receiver. These usually transfer proprietary or restricted information. They are directed toward a specific goal of improving the technical capability of the receiving nation. Typically, this is an iterative process: the receiver requests specific information, applies it, develops new findings, and then requests further information. This process is normally continued for several years, until the receiver demonstrates the desired capability.[5]

"Passive" relationships, involving short-term sales or transfers of information or products already disseminated widely, were found to be ineffective technology-transfer mechanisms.

The difference between active and passive transfers is of central political importance to the Soviet leadership. Active transfer implies a long-term, intimate foreign involvement in important areas of the Soviet economy. The traditional insulation of the Soviet economy from outsiders would thus be breached not only economically by an expanding reliance on imported goods and services representing foreign technology, but also politically by opening the knowledge of, and even participation in, the decision-making process to Western managers.

Experience of effective technology transfer elsewhere suggests not only a selective reform of economic administration, but also pressures to redirect priorities in resource allocation.

Japan is often cited as the country that most effectively utilizes the active transfer of foreign, especially American, technology. Japanese ability to absorb, diffuse, and adapt Western technology has been said to depend on a number of factors now relevant to Soviet plans:

1. developed infrastructure, such as transportation and communication facilities
2. trained workers, engineers, and managers
3. domestic research and development capabilities to assist in adaptation and exploitation of new technologies
4. domestic supplies or convenient foreign sources of vital raw materials
5. domestic or foreign markets for goods produced with the imported technology
6. willingness to promote active mechanisms, with extensive contacts between domestic and foreign technical and managerial personnel
7. flexible domestic industrial organization, including a managerial system that provides incentives to innovate, minimize costs, and take risks
8. information about the technological state of the arts in foreign industries
9. complementary industries and a reliable supply system to provide necessary inputs for new industries
10 effective patent services, quality standards, and technical documentation centers
11. financial institutions to assist in establishment of new industries[6]

Interaction of Economic and Political Systems

Carl Linden notes in chapter 2 of this book that Lenin designed the Soviet party-state to negate the nether forces of democracy and nationalism: "They have chained the forces of industrialism to the political aims of the party-state, seeking to prevent 'economics' from gaining sway over 'politics' and 'ideology'."

The current Soviet economic strategy appears to unchain these nether forces in economic development. In order to absorb Western technology effectively, Soviet leaders have been attempting to make Soviet institutional forms more responsive to active system transfer requirements. Some examples to illustrate this approach are: (1) the Kama truck plant association seeming to operate effectively outside the Ministry of Auto Industries; (2) the Ministry of Chemical Industries dealing directly with foreign suppliers rather than exclusively through the state trading monopoly; and (3) the economic sectors of the Central Committee seeming to intervene more in the planning and economic policy process.

The party is the most important institutional barrier to the successful accommodation of Western technological systems into the Soviet economy. On the one hand, it is probably essential that the top party leaders, such as Brezhnev and Kosygin, intervene on a continual basis to make Western technology transfers effective. Yet, on the other hand, it is equally important that the lower level party and industrial managers committed to traditional methods not be allowed to control or intervene in the operation of the transplanted Western systems.

What appears to be occurring is a centralization of party intervention at the top party level—the Central Committee and Council of Ministers—and a disengagement of the regional and local party from Western connected enterprises. The CPSU Central Committee even appears to be directly involved in the formulation of long-term economic plans.[7] In Eastern Europe, especially in Hungary, presumably under the Soviet policy umbrella, the role of the party in important export-related industries has been significantly changed. Illustrative is the special role in Hungary of the Corn-Production System and State Farm *Babolna*, directed by Robert Burgert and the transport and agricultural equipment production enterprises and *RABU* (Railroad, Carriage, and Machine Works), under the direction of Ede Horvath. In Poland and Bulgaria there are similar Western technology-management enclaves. The unique independence of these enterprises from party and economic bureaucratic controls suggests how far similar Western-connected enterprises in the USSR might go in the interests of efficiency in production and securing foreign markets.

Likewise it should be noted that the military are often among those most supportive of technological improvement and the effective use of Western technology. This may seem surprising in that the military might be expected to suffer if resource priorities were shifted to accommodate technological change. If the resource-demanding function of Soviet imports of Western technology exceeds the resource-releasing function, the traditional Soviet high priority investment sectors may be affected. For example, resources needed to complement technology imports in active systems may have to be diverted from military programs. If so, the traditional party advocates of a high priority for military spending would undoubtedly exercise their considerable political power to impede change. They might more readily accept the long-run utility of a more modern energy base, but not at the expense of short-run cuts in key military programs. They might, however, be partially assuaged by the gains in administrative power over high technology civilian projects offsetting their loss in resource priority. This would be more attractive if top leadership policy seemed to give them no better alternative.

Largely because they have occupied a preferred position in terms of resource allocation, Soviet defense industries tend to operate more efficiently than those in the civilian sector. One approach to shifting domestic priorities while retaining the efficiency of the defense industries would be to expand the role of military industrial managers to include increased management of civilian activities. Premier Kosygin noted in 1971 that an increasing share of Soviet consumer goods were being produced in defense plants.[8] Likewise, the important role of military builders in the construction of civilian projects has long been established.[9] Military managerial and engineering expertise could presumably be used more widely to improve civilian industries, including Western-assisted projects. Such an approach, while it may be considered risky for domestic political reasons, could aid in using new technologies more effectively.

Whatever the appropriate or necessary institutional and political adjustments, a new economic strategy of selective interdependence appears to have been adopted. The Soviets have always had problems in effectively managing projects involving Western technology. To improve this situation, Soviet planners have shown increasing interest in Western management techniques, such as quality control, production scheduling, and marketing skills. However, traditional Soviet technology transfer mechanisms have not provided arrangements for facilitating the absorption of Western management technique.

The Soviet leadership's awareness of these and other problems have led them to consider more flexible arrangements for importing Western technology. The traditional Soviet approach has been giving way to a modified systems approach to technology transfer. The new approach is characterized by: (1) a long-term or continuous connection; (2) complex or project-oriented management and distribution; (3) systems-related construction production, management, and distribution; (4) Western involvement both in country and at home in the training and the decision-making process.

Perhaps a mixed economy is possible in the Soviet Union or the Eastern countries. But to return to the old Leninist notion of the Soviet society under siege, if the invader—in this case Western systems of technology—once breaches the defense, the defense may be lost. Certainly, extensive expectations for systemic changes are not in order. However, the most successful and receptive system to accommodate the much needed Western technology is quite different from the existing, traditional Soviet system. If the Soviets are to maximize for economic reasons, the change may be most costly for the political and ideological system they have held so important for so long.

Notes

1. John Hardt, "Soviet Commercial Relations and Political Change," in R. Bauer, ed., *The Interaction of Economics and Foreign Policy* (Charlottesville, Va.: University of Virginia Press, 1975).

2. John Hardt and George Holliday, "Technology Transfer and Change in the Soviet Economic System," in F. Fleron, ed., *Technology and Communist Culture* (New York: Praeger, 1978).

3. *Pravda*, December 17, 1975, and March 7, 1976.

4. Robert W. Campbell, "Issues in Soviet R & D: The Energy Case," *Soviet Economy in a New Perspective* (Washington, D.C.: Government Printing Office, 1976); Joseph Berliner, "Prospects for Technological Progress," in *Soviet Economy in a New Perspective*, pp. 431-46; Philip Hanson, "The Diffusion of Imported Technology in the U.S.S.R." and Robert W. Campbell, "Technological Levels in the Soviet Energy Sector," NATO Conference, March 1976 (publication forthcoming).

5. U.S. Department of Defense, *An Analysis of Export Control of U.S. Technology—A D.O.D. Perspective* (Washington, D.C., 1976), pp. 9-14.

6. George Holliday, *Technology Transfer and US-USSR Cooperative Exchange Programs* (Washington, D.C.: House of Representatives International Relations Committee, 1977).

7. B. Gostev, "Economic Strategy of the Party," *Ekonomicheskaya Gazeta*, no. 14, 1976, pp. 3ff.

8. *Pravda*, April 7, 1971.

9. A.J. Romashko, *Military Builders in the Construction Projects of Moscow* (Moscow: Ministry of Defense Press, 1972).

5

The Impact of CMEA Integration on Social Change in Eastern Europe: The Case of Hungary's New Economic Mechanism

Arpad Abonyi and Ivan J. Sylvain

Since the end of World War II, Eastern Europe has experienced significant social transformation. The degree and quality of this change differs significantly within the region, but there is no doubt that it has been vast and irreversible. Following the Soviet model, the Leninist regimes of Eastern Europe have actively sought to lead and control this process. Indeed, controlled change is the essence of this model, and one of its primary goals.

The systemic requirement that the party leads and controls the whole process of social transformation and its aftermath has produced countervailing tendencies in both Eastern Europe and the Soviet Union at domestic and regional levels. It has been made even more acute in the context of dissimilar national attributes. Once the extensive stage of industrialization had been passed, the demands of continued economic progress came into conflict with the requirement of party control. Innovative reforms in the search for greater efficiency needed for intensive economic growth, as in Czechoslovakia, have served to undermine the party's leading role and its claim to be the modernizing agent. At the same time, in the absence of popular consensus on its power monopoly, the party increasingly seeks to provide compensation by producing the material rewards that accrue from greater economic efficiency.

In Eastern Europe this paradox of efficiency and control is

exacerbated by the autarkic logic of the Soviet model. Development by strictly national economic means was never a real possibility for most of the small states of the region and is progressively becoming less so. National development strategies must increasingly emphasize international sources of growth, efficiency, and control.

All the states of the region have sought a shortcut to efficiency through imports of Western technology and have attempted to overcome national deficiencies through newly adopted regional development strategies. Both pose major practical problems. The diffusion of Western technology complements regional strategies, but through the introduction of capitalist elements, it challenges the Soviet model of development as well as Marxist-Leninist values, thus undermining the party's prescriptions for society. Regional strategies, with their reliance on external sources of growth, introduce new questions into central management policies. For example, who will control change and in what direction? Will the original mobilization system be adapted to regional administration? If so, what will be the effect on domestic progress?

Since 1968, and especially since the adoption of the Comprehensive Program in 1971, the evolution of regional policies affecting members of the Council for Mutual Economic Assistance (CMEA)—particularly economic strategies, institutional networks, ideological guidelines, and the relationship between national elites—has had considerable impact on the forces of social change in Eastern Europe. Determined by ubiquitous Soviet power as much as by regional asymmetries, these policies serve to control and channel the previously generated national momentum for change. Such change has either been totally reversed, as in Czechoslovakia, arrested and channeled, as in Hungary, or incorporated, as in the case of East German reforms, into what is now the new CMEA "integration model." The new model reaffirms the value of Soviet experience at the regional level; enhances the systemic imperative of political control; and constrains national potential for change of member states. Because of their increasing impact on domestic conditions, CMEA policies must now be analyzed as an important aspect of the process of social change in Eastern Europe.

We will therefore attempt to show how the structure of regional relationships can affect the national development of CMEA's East European members. A discussion of the dimensions and current phase of social change is followed by an analysis of regional political and economic relationships. A case study of the changing nature of the Hungarian New Economic Mechanism (NEM) is used to illustrate how the emerging CMEA integration strategies have modified national options for change.

Social Mobilization, National Development, and Social Change

The notion of change is defined here as "the successive differences over time of a persisting identity,"[1] in this case the centralized administration of societies in Eastern Europe. These differences can be categorized according to how they affect the object of study.

First, identity is affected by change that "occurs when a society, as a result of disturbances induced either by internal developments or impact from without, changes its structural form."[2] This is known as *change of type* and occurred in Eastern Europe when capitalist, or in some cases "pre-capitalist," societies were transformed after 1945 into Marxist-Leninist regimes, according to institutions and principles *diffused* from the Soviet Union. The structural form of such societies is identified by the following key political and economic relationships: they are ruled by a Communist party, which enjoys monopoly of political power exercised on the basis of democratic centralism; the party, which is composed of a narrow elite, is centrally organized; and all forms of societal relations are subordinated to it in hierarchical structure. Lower units in this structure are strictly subordinated to higher-level party bodies whose decisions are binding. This effectively circumscribes the autonomy of lower-level units or actors.

Because Leninist regimes are dedicated to transforming society on the basis and toward the goals of Marxism-Leninism, they take an active leading role.[3] They mobilize resources in society, converting them from private to public purposes. By aggregating and controlling interests, each state party is instrumental in shaping the attitudes and opinions of society, including those towards the CMEA.[4] Through central controls all aspects of social activity are politicized, and private interests, political opposition, and conflicting ideologies are suppressed.

This political structure is mirrored in centrally planned economic administration. The economy is vertically integrated under a centralized, bureaucratic, decision-making authority, which subordinates lower levels in a chain of more or less detailed planning. Planning itself is also vertically controlled.[5] It implements the political-economic goals of the powerful decision-making organs at the top of the hierarchy.

Second, differences and readjustments may occur without affecting the structural form of society.[6] Thus, among others, Kenneth Jowitt, Mark Field, and Zvi Gitelman have shown that it is possible to isolate and describe various phases in the development of an identity still essentially a Marxist-Leninist society.[7] Jowitt clearly delineates such phases as transformation, consolidation, and inclusion.[8] CMEA's regimes began as revolutionary movements that achieved power, not necessarily through violent means, ostensibly to correct the wrongs of the past and build a new society according to a given ideology. Their initial concern was transforming a once capitalist society into a socialist one based on Marxist-Leninist ideology. Having achieved power, these regimes' main task was to consolidate their power and implement their goals for the future. This meant the elimination of certain groups from society through violence, if necessary, and the massive mobilization of resources for the purpose of economic development.

Reliance on coercion during the consolidation phase tended to atomize society and isolate the party from it. In the inclusion phase, the party has sought to legitimize its exercise of power through greater use of persuasion, to facilitate the integration of the masses and emergent technical elites into the Marxist-Leninist society. In so doing, an appeal to nationalistic aims has been designed to bolster new socialist states by utilizing a historically rooted sense of patriotism. In addition, promises of delayed gratification have been replaced by real efforts at making consumer goods available. This emphasis on consumerism contributed to the emergence of technical elites needed to manage an economy of greater complexity and functional specificity, whose cooperation (hence consultation) has been increasingly required by the party's strategic elite.[9]

The political goals and economic requirements of the inclusion phase are intertwined. The political requisite, that of greater legitimization, is complemented by the economic requisite, that of greater rationalization. This has been made necessary by the failure of the Soviet model to facilitate transition to an intensive growth pattern once extensive sources of growth, the ever-increasing inputs of capital and labor, have become progressively less viable. At the same time, the directive nature of the planning system has hindered the development of new technologies and qualitative improvements in production required for intensive growth. The system made it progressively more difficult not only to shift resources into more technologically intensive consumer industries, but even to continue the emphasis on the old priorities of industrialization.

In order to resolve these problems of the inclusion phase, East European regimes have resorted to various economic reforms. Radoslav Selucky has categorized them three ways: administrative, mixed or hybrid, and market socialism.[10] The first aims at improving the command system, which is considered basically still viable. The hybrid form combines centralized macroeconomic decision making with some degree of microeconomic managerial autonomy according to market-type regulations. This continues planned direction of the economy but attempts to incorporate market efficiency into the plan. The third category is the most radical in the CMEA context. Assuming that central command planning is irretrievably inefficient, it permits the interplay of market forces, with the plan relegated to providing only the basic indicators for amelioration of the social effects of a market-directed economy.[11] The last type of reform may mean more than a simple adjustment as it may unleash the forces that change the structural identity characterstic of a Marxist-Leninist society. More specifically, if decison making is decentralized and prices replace planners' preferences as economic criteria, what has become of the party's leading role? Under these circumstances the regional definition of what constitutes a Marxist-Leninist society becomes crucial to the direction of change.

The precarious balance emerging from attempts to maintain control and to implement systemic changes at the national level "must not jeopardize the existence of some form of international Leninist regime community."[12] As the Soviet party elite reserves the right to define what a genuine Leninist regime is, and, within broad limits, how it should behave, the sine qua non of a CMEA party's acceptability remains the ability to maintain its leading role. Because certain reform programs undermine this role, the national strategic elites of Eastern Europe are continually caught between Soviet demands to conform to Leninist norms and internally generated pressures for pragmatic systemic change.

The national strategic elites, however, are not perfect middle-men because any decline in the party's leading role means personal loss of power for them. Thus they have reason to conform to Soviet-defined Leninist norms and to require the external support without which their position might deteriorate. To varying degrees, therefore, the national strategic elites are penetrating agents that "carry out certain functions on behalf of foreign interests; in return they enjoy a privileged, . . . dominant and hegemonic position within their own societies based largely on economic, political or military support from abroad."[13]

On the other hand, to the extent that East European political elites are genuine *national* communists, their policies are constrained by the structure of regional relationships in the Soviet bloc. Military intervention is the most extreme constraint, but is only used as a last resort when other political and economic means have failed to induce conformity. The imposition of the Soviet development model has produced a regional interdependence that significantly adds to the means available to limit national alternatives for change without resorting to military threat or force.

Web of Regional Ties as Dependence

The enforced adoption of the Soviet growth strategy at the national level has produced a situation "in which the economy of certain countries [in East Europe] is conditioned by the development and expansion of another country [USSR] to which the former is subject."[14] This relationship is an asymmetrical one through which the Soviet Union is able to condition the opportunities and behavior of national political and economic structures in CMEA to meet its own needs and purposes. Because the reverse is not true, that is to say East European members of CMEA do not have this same *power* over the Soviet Union, this relational inequality of one-way domination can be called dependence.[15]

The Soviet model has proved less than adequate for Eastern Europe. Imbalanced, autarkic, extensively generated economic growth has been appropriate for the Soviet Union, with its huge domestic market, large reserves of labor, and rich natural resources. East European countries, however, had neither, and the adoption of the Soviet model resulted in predictable economic difficulties. Both scarcities and surpluses developed in East European economies. An attempt at autarky that involved proliferation of import-saving heavy industries, regardless of comparative advantage, exhausted domestic supplies of labor and resources. The low quality goods thus produced were not competitive on Western markets, thereby creating domestic surpluses. Combined with the lack of raw materials, the particular predicament of scarcities leading to surpluses has been more pronounced in countries more heavily dependent on foreign imports, particularly imports of energy.

In general, imbalances of the autarkic type of development resulted in low volume of foreign trade (used by central planners to balance off domestic surpluses and scarcities),[16] and a characteristic trade pattern. First, unable to generate intensive growth internally, CMEA as a whole is dependent upon imports of Western technology,[17] although its ability to do so has been severely limited by scarcity of primary goods available for export as well as by the noncompetitive character of its manufactured products. Second, the pattern serves to perpetuate inequalities in the region and intensifies the dependency of the smaller partners on the Soviet Union. Countries with industrial experience and appropriately skilled labor, primarily Czechoslovakia and East Germany (GDR), but to a lesser extent also Poland and Hungary, maintain their technological lead but at the price of orienting their economies to Soviet development requirements.[18] This has retarded their ability to produce industrial goods competitive in the West, forcing them increasingly to depend on the Soviet market for the disposal of surplus goods in exchange for indispensable raw materials, a pattern of exchange favoring bilateral ties as well as dependence on the strongest partner. The structure of Bulgarian trade is dissimilar, but it is even more closely tied to the Soviet Union. Only Romania's position is unique, because it can still rely on the luxury of its own extensive sources of growth,[19] thus lessening the dependence.

Finally, the Soviet Union does not depend on East European inputs to sustain development. The Soviet core area's natural autarky and economic size, combined with the command economic model, lend it considerable decision-making freedom in its relations with CMEA countries and ensure Soviet domination of each industrial sector within CMEA. This is maximized by bilateralism, also a natural outgrowth of command planning.[20] Because trade requires coordination of national production plans, negotiations are carried on bilaterally; each European country's agents must deal with the Soviet agents separately.

The net result of these intraregional imbalances is entrenchment of Soviet hegemony. The industrial growth of smaller CMEA members becomes tied to expanding extraction of Soviet raw materials, in return for which they must also expand exports of machinery to the Soviet market, or invest, despite tight funds, in its development. Furthermore, the bilateral character of negotiations place each East European nation in a disadvantageous bargaining position. Because the results intimately affect the structure and success of their own development plans, pressures on the penetrated national elites are maximized from above and below.

Maintaining the structure of these relationships, however, has not been without costs for the Soviet Union. Despite the considerable variation and obfuscation of unrealistic trade prices, machinery (the key East European export) has enjoyed advantageous terms of trade in the region.[21] This may be seen as an economic cost of maintaining political influence, as trade relations with Eastern Europe progressively interfere with Soviet attempts to capitalize on radically altered energy prices in the West in exchange for technology.[22] This Western competition, in turn, makes Soviet demands for East European aid in expanding its raw material base and for improvement of the quality of machinery traded to it more immediately effective.

As seen earlier, Western technology is desirable in all

command-planned economies. It is, nevertheless, viewed as a mixed blessing by the Soviet and East European strategic elites. The effective use of Western technology may require use of Western experts and their entrepreneurial or managerial skills. The resultant package may have a considerable "demonstration effect,"[23] strengthening forces for change that in turn threaten to undermine the leading role of the party. To neutralize this latent threat, the Soviet Union seeks to increase regional control over CMEA relations.

Western technology imports are thus tolerated as a short-term strategy by the Soviet and East European elites only in so far as they serve to overcome problems of the intensive phase of development; *once* this is achieved, the need for foreign technology imports will decline, as will the danger of contamination it carries. Since the goal of economic development is shared by the elites as well as the technocrats, the reformers, and the masses, the regional cooperation designed to facilitate it is an effective target for mobilizing the human and material resources of CMEA.

Indeed, some form of regional cooperation is required for successful intensive development. In CMEA this is called the "internationalization of the forces of production" and primarily refers to international division of labor, pooling of research and development efforts, and reaping economies of scale on a regional level.[24] But because of asymmetrical relationships in CMEA, the resulting structural changes in patterns of production and trade are not distributed equally and thereby enhance the role of the Soviet penetrating actor.

Fears of just such an outcome have dominated the history of attempts at regional cooperation. Both Romania and Bulgaria have opposed Soviet proposals of international division of labor within CMEA. Both feared that it would lock them into position as the permanent primary materials producers for the region. Of the two alternatives to multilateral cooperation, marketization and supranational planning, the first has been advocated by Hungary and the second by the Soviet Union.[25]

The first view has been that the patent inadequacies of command planning for foreign trade and international comparisons require marketization; the second, that the logic of the system requires supranational planning.

Neither type of multilateral cooperation is ideally suited to the CMEA. As studies of Third World integration have observed, the market tends to amplify existing regional inequalities and can reproduce global patterns of dependence within an area through "backwash effects." Some form of regional planning has been offered as a means of reducing these inequalities.[26] Planning, however, is not immune to the problem of existing asymmetries. If planners' preferences stress comparative advantage, structural inequality will still result. It is hardly surprising, therefore, that East Germany has defended the principle of considering factor costs for CMEA planning, while Romania has been generally opposed to it.[27] Moreover, the type of planning used will affect the structural outcome. Radoslav Selucky has argued that, given "pure" command planning:

> If . . . bilateral cooperation is to be replaced by multilateral cooperation based on the gradually increasing degree of joint command planning, the sum total of various national command economic systems is but a supra-national command system, or, in other words, the sum total of national hierarchical pyramids creates a single international hierarchical pyramid. Because of the extension of vertical relationships to the supra-national decison-making body, national central power-political organs cease to be exclusively top organs and become merely organs of secondary importance.[28]

A supranational organ can compensate for regional inequalities if its decision-making power is more or less evenly distributed among members. Given the structure of CMEA relationships however, such an organ would only serve as a mechanism to fuse national economies of East European members into that of the Soviet Union.[29]

Even if no supranational organization is created, the logic of planning requires matching organizational structures and does not tolerate administrative deviance. Just as an inconvertible currency hinders free trade, alternative economic structures hinder planned cooperation. The more this cooperation becomes significant for national economies, the less tolerable becomes organizational deviation.

> Organic and consistent mutual tying in of national plans will quite obviously become possible, only if it rests on joint planning activity effected at various levels of economic management. The point here is essentially to bring closer the forms and methods of domestic planning and joint planning activity. Up to now there has been a very considerable gap in these.[30]

Thus regional strategy based on a common plan requires increasingly common administrative structures. Because of the direction of dependence in the region, it is logical to assume that the Soviet Union will set the pattern for these structures. Unlike its junior East European partners, it can bear the increased costs of maintaining the command planning system without resorting to significant reorganization. In practice this means that greater integration will restrict economic reform alternatives in CMEA in a way that favors the conservative administrative type and seriously impedes the emergence or evolution of the hybrid and market-socialism reforms that call for decentralization.

The incompatibility of a decentralized model and a command planning system is exemplified by Hungary's NEM in the context of CMEA integration. When NEM was first introduced in 1968, its ambitious and even radical hybrid program was an innovative attempt to solve problems of the inclusion phase. Because it remained intact after the Warsaw Pact invasion of Czechoslovakia, NEM had at least a modicum of legitimacy among other members of CMEA including the Soviet Union and has created a lot of interest and optimism in the West. Also, the appearance of NEM closely coincided with discussions of domestic reforms and meaningful alternative integrative strategies for CMEA. With the success of conservative strategies at the regional level, however, there has been a parallel retrenchment of NEM domestically, demonstrating the potential impact CMEA policies have on the direction of social change in East Europe.

Domestic Change and Regional Constraints: The Case of Hungarian Reforms

The 1956 Hungarian Revolution demonstrated the futility of the party's efforts to consolidate its position by coercion that led only to popular alienation and political instability. Soviet military intervention restored the party to power, but long-term instability and alienation remained. Clearly the old methods had failed, and the newly renamed Hungarian Socialist Workers' Party (HSWP) had to offer the people positive incentives. This meant disassociating the HSWP from the discredited Rákosi regime and attempting to build new forms of legitimacy.

Thus, following a brief period of reconsolidation (1956-58), Janos Kádár, the Soviet-installed leader of the resurrected party, has charted a program of relative depoliticization and economic improvement. The role of ideology was de-emphasized under Kádár's now familiar slogan, "All who are not against us are with us," which signified the party's willingness to decrease its active intervention in daily life in return for passive acceptance of its leading role. The simultaneous decrease in ideological rigidity and appeal to economic gain more closely suited the Hungarian political culture.[31] The new course did not mean that the goal of a Marxist-Leninist society was abandoned; rather it represented an indirect attempt at Leninist socialization by demonstrating the efficacy of a socialist economy for individual well-being and overall development.

The emphasis on economic prosperity required alterations

in the structure and performance of the command planning system, and the HSWP began by co-opting and consulting technocratic elites. First, Kádár strengthened the party's ability to lead a reform program by increasing the role of innovators within its own ranks such as Jenö Fock, premier and Politburo member, and Lajos Fehér, Politburo member for agriculture. Second, the HSWP inducted technocrats into both its upper and lower echelons at the expense of more dogmatic cadres. Foremost among the newly co-opted elite was Rezsö Nyers, who became an alternate member of the Politburo at the Eighth Party Congress in November 1962.[32] Through 1962 and 1963, he formulated economic reform plans and defended them to the HSWP's dogmatic wing. This was reinforced by studies critical of central planning under the Rákosi regime.[33]

To resolve differences of opinion, the party's Central Committee decided, in December 1964, to review the entire system of national economic planning and management. Under Nyers' supervision, eleven work groups staffed by 130 experts were set up to study the economy and to draft reform proposals.[34] In May 1966, the party's Central Committee unanimously approved the principles of the New Economic Mechanism, which became effective in January 1968. The apparent unanimity behind NEM, however, did not mean a complete victory for the reformers. The principles of the reform program reflected a compromise; dogmatists were silenced but not routed.

This study does not intend to document the need for a shift to an intensive phase of development in Hungary. This has been extensively dealt with elsewhere.[35] It is sufficient to note here that this resource- and labor-poor country was subject to all the ills of command-planned industrialization and was heavily dependent on foreign trade for economic growth (a 2 percent increase in foreign trade turnover meant a 1 percent growth in national income).[36] In attempting to promote consumerism, economic efficiency, and an improved position in world markets, NEM sought to introduce market-type microeconomic regulators with the plan reduced to a supplementary macroeconomic tool.

Under the new system the plan ostensibly ceased to be a *direct* regulator of the economy, instructing each individual enterprise in detail how to carry out their functions. Instead, the planners set the parameters of *indirect* regulators, which were designed to simulate a market environment.[37] This entailed substantial transfer of decision-making authority to enterprise managers. Commensurately, the role of the National Planning Office was limited to setting targets for and coordinating overall economic development. Ministries also assumed new functions. They were to direct technical development, supervise and control economic efficiency of enterprises, and stimulate domestic and international cooperation, rather than act as the second level in a command hierarchy.[38]

In principle then, indirect regulators were to be used in two ways: (1) as policy instruments to maintain stability and to control overall direction of the economy and (2) as the guidelines for enterprise managers to implement production targets in conformity with general, party-defined norms but with maximum economic efficiency. Under these circumstances, the enterprise became the most important economic unit in society; in consequence, its legal independence and rights were enhanced. Enterprises were empowered to retain a portion of profits for reinvestment, to consult newly established market research organization, and to engage directly in foreign trade. Ultimately this reorganization was designed to create a competitive, sales-oriented environment.[39]

Four basic categories of regulators were employed to simulate this environment. First, the architects of NEM realized that it was not enough to increase responsibilities for the enterprise manager without providing incentives. They therefore employed a system of bonuses based on a share of enterprise profits. Income regulators were also extended to workers' wages. On one hand, workers too received a percentage of profits, albeit a proportionally smaller amount.

On the other hand, enterprises were taxed for increased wage bills in order to induce more efficient use of labor.[40]

Second, in order to promote efficient use of investment funds, a series of financial regulators were employed. In addition to retention of some enterprise profits, bank credits were made available for circulating capital and expansion of industrial facilities. Government financing was retained for large scale projects.[41]

Third, a reform program based on market-type regulators necessitated attempts to make prices more meaningful. In contrast to the previously unrealistic rigid fixed price system, they were now to reflect the value of capital and labor inputs. At the same time, prices were also to act as signals of the market, mirroring supply and demand relationships. To these ends (1) the turnover taxes were shifted to the producers; (2) consumer prices were reduced somewhat and industrial prices increased; and (3) a four-tier price system was created to allow some fluctuation without planner control or approval.[42]

Finally, these more realistic prices were combined with a set of regulators designed to stimulate efficient and profitable foreign trade. NEM introduced a price multiplier that was a uniform conversion ratio based on the average cost of producing certain goods in particular industries of the domestic economy. The multiplier linked the Hungarian forint to the Western market in dollars and to CMEA in transferable rubles, enabling enterprises to relate their pricing structure to international cost conditions.[43] The multiplier, however, still left many Hungarian industries inefficient. In order to compensate, NEM permitted allocation of state subsidies to increase enterprise efficiency. In addition, the Ministry of Foreign Trade and other central agencies retained the right to amend the exchange rate, taxes, and duties in conformity with the external targets of the national economic plan. Also, the government could use investment and credit policies to favor the development of productive capacities designed for foreign trade.[44]

Enterprise autonomy combined with efforts to create

meaningful prices in a system of indirect planning marks NEM as a radical hybrid reform. Technocrat-inspired, NEM also had overall national political appeal because of the shift of general economic priorities to consumer-related industries. Initial national acceptance was not enough to guarantee success, however, because Hungary's particular trade linkages to international markets required further adjustments. These were sought by adopting Western methods of market efficiency. The drawback here was that while enhancing trade with the West, these impeded economic relations with CMEA, other members of which remained centrally directed. At the same time Hungary's condition of economic dependence on CMEA, and particularly the Soviet Union,[45] remained unaltered.

The CMEA trade pattern also posed significant obstacles to the operation of NEM. First, centralized bilateral agreements, characteristic of CMEA trade were concluded by respective trade ministries. When, after the introduction of NEM, managers took part in negotiations on the Hungarian side, they had no direct contact with their counterparts in other CMEA countries and had to deal through the medium of Foreign Trade Enterprises. Moreover, bilateralism often entailed arbitrary decision making. In certain cases, trade did not materialize from planned negotiations, but resulted from brief ministerial meetings where neither managers nor Foreign Trade Enterprise representatives were present.[46] In order to make such informal agreements meaningful, the Hungarian National Planning Office had to issue new directives undermining the effective use of economic regulators.[47]

Second, while Hungary was endeavoring to simulate a market environment by using scarcity prices, other members were not. The foreign trade multiplier helped the Hungarian manager relate his cost of production to meaningful Western prices but was of little use in trade with CMEA members who still clung to the artificial fixed prices, reviewed only every five years. As the fixed foreign trade prices did not reflect the value of wage and capital costs embodied in production, they failed to differentiate between the unequal value of national labor as well as the uneven levels of efficiency inherent in a very diverse region.[48] This meant that less developed countries received the same fixed prices as their technically advanced counterparts, even though their costs of production were higher. Because regional price signals were so unreliable, Hungarian enterprises could not be sure that their production was efficient, undermining NEM objectives of foreign trade. Fixed prices clearly subsidized the less developed members of CMEA.

Third, the shift toward consumer industries under NEM represented more than an effort to mobilize mass support for the party's program. Given Hungary's lack of raw materials, it also served as the basis for building up Hungary's comparative advantage in CMEA. Industrial parallelism in the region, however, inhibited greater international division of labor. Here again, Hungary's interests diverged from the less developed CMEA members.

The Emergence of Regional Development Strategy and the NEM: Circumscribed Alternatives

Given Hungary's economic dependence, these regional constraints had to be overcome in order for NEM to flourish. From the first then, Hungarian reformers sought to externalize their policies by arguing for reform of regional trade practices. This was not necessarily an impossible task, because since the mid-1960s there had been a general dissatisfaction with the declining rate of growth in trade among CMEA members.[49] Moreover, other reforms attempting to rationalize domestic economies stressed the issue of specialization at the regional level. Despite Khrushchev's failure to introduce a planned socialist division of labor for CMEA in 1962, the inherent shortcomings of the Soviet model of development made it necessary by the mid-1960s for resource-poor countries to abandon strict autarky in favor of some form of regional cooperation.[50] Such specialization could augment domestic supplies of raw materials. It could also help alleviate problems of intensive development by offering economies of scale through specialization without resorting to significant economic reform. Finally, in early 1968 when NEM was introduced, it naturally complemented the Czechoslovakian hybrid reform program.

Hungarian reformers conducted an aggressive campaign to convince other CMEA members of the need to adopt regional policies complementary to effective implementation of NEM. Indeed, as early as 1967 the Hungarians and Czechoslovaks were actively considering bilateral trade liberalization. By the introduction of NEM in January 1968, they had signed an agreement covering "free trade commodities,"[51] and Hungary envisioned similar relations with Yugoslavia. These early successes were swept away by the Soviet-led invasion of Czechoslovakia. Nevertheless, this setback did not immediately undermine the Hungarian campaign. Although it had lost an ally, NEM gained credibility by surviving the invasion.

Both within CMEA institutions, notably in council sessions, and through a series of official, critical publications, the Hungarians continued to press for their revisionist policies.[52] In essence they were proposing a market-type regional integration scheme based on enterprise autonomy under indirect planning, and meaningful prices requiring a convertible international currency. This scheme was best articulated by Antal Ápro, Rezsö Nyers, and Tibor Kiss. Ápro, a long-time Politburo member and Hungarian representative to CMEA, was the first, following the introduction of NEM, to stress dissatisfaction with overcentralized planning in trade relations at the regional level. In particular he called for increased enterprise autonomy under the loose control of the CMEA policymaking organ.[53] Nyers characterized the Hungarian position as the gradual introduction of a regionally integrated yet controlled market.[54]

Kiss, a professional economist, member of state committees, and an important advisor on economic policy, provided the most scholarly and substantive statement of Hungary's position. Despite Czechoslovakia's setback, he hoped that the free trade agreement previously signed between the two countries would be adopted in the form of a CMEA-level economic customs union based on the principles of a regulated market. He wanted abolition of barriers to exchange of goods and free movement of capital and labor. On the one hand, he argued, this customs-union format would foster economic efficiency; on the other, it would most adequately protect the national sovereignty of smaller CMEA members, given their need to cooperate under changing economic conditions. A customs union did not require command planning at the regional level. Its flexibility permitted a partial transfer of sovereignty, enabling small countries to influence regional economic decisions without the transfer of political sovereignty required by regional supranational planning. The flexibility was predicated in the indirect nature of planning as envisioned by NEM.[55]

Hungarian proposals on a customs union were designed to protect NEM, but their implementation would have affected the internal economic mechanisms of other members. Market-type regulators of a customs union would make it incumbent upon other CMEA members to adapt their domestic structures and goals to the pattern of NEM. Thus the Hungarian position demonstrates that the issues of integration and domestic reforms cannot be isolated.

Other nations also realized that the type of regional integrative strategy adopted for CMEA could either reinforce or threaten their own economic mechanisms. In particular, East Germany felt that adoption of regional policies based on hybrid reforms would threaten their own conservative attempt at restructuring the nature of direct planning. It argued that the Hungarian reforms contained "revisionist" elements, and quite emphatically warned CMEA members that spontaneity and market socialism should not be tolerated if they wanted to preserve central control.[56]

Central control was precisely what the Soviets wished to

maintain within their own system and over the future direction of the CMEA as well. The Soviets envisioned a more centralized integration scheme based on plan coordination and eventual joint planning.[57] Their sponsorship of this type of integration was critical. For the USSR alone had enough economic leverage to undermine NEM by insisting on centralized bilateral negotiation and threatening to withhold vital raw materials.

The Soviet Union was supported by its traditional conservative allies, East Germany and Bulgaria,[58] and by 1970 the severely disciplined and reconstituted Czechoslovakian regime also called for regional plan coordination.[59] Of the remaining two East European members of CMEA, only Poland favored elements of the Hungarian proposal. Romania, on the other hand, resented any form of integration, fearing diminution of its national sovereignty.[60] Moreover, the Romanians, too, found little comfort in the implications of the Hungarian reforms, because they sought to maintain a centrally directed economy.

Despite their isolation, the Hungarian reformers continued their aggressive campaign right up until the twenty-fourth CMEA Council session in May 1970, which affirmed that integration was to be based upon the principle of plan coordination and authorized preparation of a program to implement this type of strategy.[61] Following this, the Hungarians were forced onto the defensive. Nevertheless, they only abandoned advocation of a customs union for the region after a special CMEA conference held in Budapest, November 1970.[62] From then on, they only sought to ameliorate the effects of impending regional plan coordination, which was officially inaugurated at the twenty-fifth CMEA Council session in July 1971 and entitled the Comprehensive Program for Integration.[63]

The Comprehensive Program reflected divergent national interests and policy alternatives. Indeed, it appeared to be a *compromise program*. Hungarian and Polish interests were recognized by a call for the study of currency reforms. Also it permitted a limited increase in enterprise autonomy by allowing them to join newly legitimized regional economic organizations. Romanian demands were represented by re-affirming the inviolability of national sovereignty within the integrative framework. Moreover, the long-standing fears of Bulgaria and Romania that integration would freeze their industrial development were alleviated by commitment to an intrasector division of labor. Finally, the program confirmed that international plan coordination would be the basis of regional strategy.

This compromise between centralist and reformist elements was more apparent than real, for the practical aspects of the program favored planned coordination, not market tendencies. First, although study of currency reforms was authorized, a CMEA Committee for Plan Cooperation was established also.[64] Second, membership in new middle-level regional organizations, International Economic Associations, would not necessarily enhance autonomy because national minis-terial control was still retained.[65] At best, such organizations are potential focal points for creating supranational forms of power. They duplicate at the regional level the middle echelon of control found in the domestic hierarchies of conservative administrative reforms, such as East Germany's. Third, intrasectoral specialization is dependent upon closer joint planning between interested partners. Regardless of the type of coproduction or exchange involved in this type of specializa-tion, participants would jointly have to forecast and to coordinate investment, production, and deliveries for given branches of industry. This makes the success of one national plan contingent upon another's, and limits enterprise auto-nomy by committing it to long-term arrangements. Finally, the most immediate aspect of the program was a call for joint investment projects to develop facilities for extraction and processing of raw materials. Through these projects, the Soviets hoped to improve their terms of trade by receiving East European investment, labor, and capital goods to aid development of these Soviet resources.[66] This would of course increase the dependent status of East European members in the region.

In sum, then, the Comprehensive Program represents the first stage in a gradual process that stresses stages of development in leading sectors of key industries, a process that eventually will produce a common plan as a capstone to a second or "higher" stage.[67] Indeed, this second stage may be tantamount to the supranational planning advocated by Khrushchev in 1962. This form of integration favoring administrative reforms at best put a straitjacket on Hungary's NEM and assured that the reforms had to be recentralized if the country was to be an active, cooperative member of CMEA.

Accordingly, there has been a steady retrenchment in NEM since 1971. Several authors have pointed out that domestic difficulties contributed to such recentralization.[68] Indeed, the domestic price reforms required to make NEM meaningful were never sufficiently implemented. For example, removing subsidies from basic foodstuffs was considered politically unacceptable, especially because the material benefits of NEM did not accrue evenly from management to workers. The differential benefit created powerful labor opposition to continuation of the reforms.[69] More importantly, the reforms never really created a competitive environment for Hungarian industry. Even when cost calculations showed an enterprise to be inefficient, it was subsidized rather than shut down, for in the short term, the unemployment this would have created was also politically unacceptable. In addition, overinvestment by enterprises created bottlenecks in supply linkage industries, thereby fostering economic destabilization. These domestic difficulties were exacerbated by CMEA's failure to adopt a market oriented regional strategy. In this hostile environment, it is understandable that planners would have to intervene actively and therefore limit effective development of a market regulated economy.

Not all of NEM's problems were a consequence of the

domestic and regional environments. The 1973 oil crisis enhanced the desirability of relatively cheap Soviet oil and demonstrated the need to maintain secure supplies. Moreover, the crisis exacerbated Western economic problems, further damaging NEM's fragile link with Western markets. On the one hand, attempts to buy technology merely imported Western inflation. On the other hand, decreased capitalist economic activity reduced demand for Hungarian goods and therefore increased the importance of the secure Soviet market.[70] The impact of extraregional events, however, should not be overstressed, for the gradual spread of planned integration was paralleled by steady recentralization. NEM was diffused but not completely dismantled. Moreover, its leading advocates were dismissed and replaced, but as with the dogmatists before them, not routed.

The return to administrative methods in Hungary was accompanied by the increasing success of regionally "planned" integration. First, the council's Cooperation and Planning Committee has steadily expanded its purview. In June 1973 it was directed to harmonize special sections of national five year plans dealing with integrative projects.[71] In 1974 the council committees for technology, material supply, and planning were empowered to establish priorities for CMEA's organs.[72] Finally, in June 1976, the Planning Committee gained approval for creating a single, "Draft Plan of Multilateral Integration Measures for the period of 1967-1980, which would incorporate the integration sections of every member state's national plan."[73] Up to now this committee has not been a supranational central planner. Rather, it is a means by which national planners are drawn together and bilateral agreements are produced. Second, plan coordination has expanded most noticeably in developmental projects designed to augment domestic deficiencies without requiring significant adminis-trative change in members' national economic mechanisms. Primary among these has been the establishment of joint investment projects for the extraction of raw materials: e.g.,

Kursk iron ore; Ust-Ilimsk cellulose; and the Orenburg gas pipeline.[74]

The emerging regional strategy clearly reflects the Soviet view of CMEA integration. It restricts the viability of alternative economic mechanisms by reinforcing Leninist centrally controlled organizational forms in society. Consequently, East Germany's conservative administrative reforms should become increasingly appealing. This was underscored by Soviet adoption of German-type reforms in March 1973.[75] In effect, the Soviet Union's administrative structures became compatible with all CMEA members, except Hungary, and cemented the norms for the region. Moreover, this increasing administrative homogeneity aptly suits Soviet ideological pronouncements concerning a socialist commonwealth. Since late 1972, "rapprochement and merger" have been used to characterize the relationships between socialist states. This is significant because it was previously only used to describe nationality relations in the Soviet Union itself. The fusion this implies, however, contradicts the guarantees of national sovereignty promised under integration.[76]

Although the content of this regional strategy is conservative and may have negative implications for national sovereignty, it does offer a means of resolving the "developmental trap" that has caught resource-poor East European states. They can obtain needed raw materials and achieve some economies of scale while retaining the old (Leninist-type) system. Although one can question the innovative capacity of this strategy, it does provide some benefits. For those countries that prefer it, these benefits include preservation of the command system. Clearly, however, this has created a hostile environment for the Hungarian reform and places considerable pressure on NEM to conform. Moreover, the pressure has been reinforced through bilateral relationships with its major trading partner, i.e., the USSR. Hungary's dependence on the USSR made this strategy successful.

Following the inception of the Cooperative Planning

Committee, ideological pronouncements directed against the bourgeois elements of market-type socialism, and clearly aimed at Hungary, appeared in the Soviet and East German press.[77] By December 1972, the Hungarians had recognized the "criticisms of their friends" and openly admitted the need for readjustments.[78] Perhaps a crucial factor in this reorientation was the USSR's failure to guarantee delivery of raw material shipments to Hungary, as announced by Premier Fock upon his return from Moscow in 1971.[79]

In order to secure imports of Soviet energy and raw materials, Hungary has participated in various resource development investment projects in the USSR, the profitability of which is questionable. Such participation requires transfer of already tight domestic funds and labor, reducing nationally based growth alternatives.[80] It does, however, provide security of supply, which has been especially important since the 1973 October war, and is clearly advantageous to the Soviet Union. This can be seen in Soviet renegotiation of regional prices for oil instead of waiting for the usual five-year period. Hungary was the first nation to be forced to renegotiate. It could hardly refuse, for it was heavily dependent and had itself argued for "price reform" in CMEA. There is at least circumstantial evidence for the fact that Hungary was not an accidental first choice.[81]

The new higher prices have severely affected the already poor Hungarian balance of trade, even though they are still below the world prices and loans have been made available to cover the increase. The change benefited Soviet ability to import Western technology, and therefore to demand higher quality goods from CMEA partners. Indeed, the Hungarians have complained that the Soviets have abused their new position by refusing entire shipments of their goods in order to delay deliveries during price renegotiations.[82] As Hungary, in its new position, must put up with considerable inconvenience, it understandably has turned to CMEA, and to the Soviet Union in particular, and de-emphasized growth in Western trade.[83]

Regional strategy and developments, then, required increased Hungarian administrative conformity. Although the spirit of NEM was necessarily violated by planners' intervention from its beginning, the first significant breaks occurred in 1971 under a general policy of investment restrictions that hamstrung enterprise autonomy. By November 1972, a Central Committee plenum placed six of the largest Hungarian enterprises under "special control"—and resolved to extend this to the fifty largest ones by January 1973. This was an important recentralization measure because these "essentially producer goods enterprises accounted for 50% of industrial output, 39% of the labour force, [and] 60% of the capital" in Hungary.[84] In July 1973, a party plenum reestablished a supraministerial State Planning Committee, which replaced a former committee disbanded at the outset of NEM. In particular, this new committee was made responsible for harmonizing domestic planning with international cooperation.[85] Fundamental reconsideration of NEM was announced by resolutions produced for the Eleventh Party Congress, March 1975.[86] Following a debate in the press and the party plenum in July 1975,[87] a new system of economic regulators was produced which became effective in January 1976. Although this new policy claimed adherence to the principles of NEM, its restrictive, directive nature stressed planning at the expense of market and reduced enterprise autonomy. Retrenchment has not, however, completely removed all the mechanisms designed to enhance micro-efficiency in the short run. For example, one and two year plans are no longer state laws but are used primarily for forecasting.[88] The renewed conservative orientation has emphasized medium- and long-term planning that closely conforms to CMEA strategies.

Recentralizing the administration of NEM's regulators was accompanied by the demotion of important reformers. Nyers and Fehér were both removed from their secretarial positions in March 1974, one year before their removal from the Politburo. Nyers lost his post because he was not "flexible" enough on the issue of retrenchment. He was replaced by Karoly Németh, who now assumed responsibility for questions of economic management. Németh, who joined the conservative voices warning against the bourgeois tendencies of reforms, represents the return of talented, yet conservative *apparatchiki* to the direction of the Hungarian economy.[89] Even more interesting is the resignation of Nyers' most ardent supporter, Premier Fock, in May 1975.

His replacement, George Lázár, may represent the "new type" of technocrat the HSWP is seeking. Lázár became premier after only five years in the Central Committee. In 1973 he obtained no less than three important posts, chairman of the National Planning Office, chairman of the new State Planning Committee, and chief representative to CMEA (replacing Antal Ápro).[90] His success demonstrates the increasing importance of planning and regional roles as avenues of success in the Hungarian elite. Other appointments made in this period confirm the demise of reformist technocrats in favor of the "new type" recruited from heavy industry and planning offices.[91] Moreover, these new postings have been popular within CMEA and particularly the USSR, exemplified by the "warm and comradely" reception Lázár received from Brezhnev, Kosygin, and Podgorny during trade negotiations in Moscow, November 1974.

Despite these transfers promoting regional conformity, NEM reformers are still in charge of economic relations with the West, and their expertise is still in demand for financial management of the economy. Because importing Western technology remains a necessary ingredient for development, the reformers retain considerable leverage.

Conclusion

There are several implications if this basically conservative orientation toward change and integration is continued. First, there is increased likelihood that recentralization in the

Hungarian case will be followed by the demise of other aberrant organizational forms, such as largely privately owned Polish agriculture. Second, the systemic problems of command-planned development have not been eliminated. They have been only partially alleviated by transferring them to the regional level. Retaining the old system intact may not provide the innovative capacity necessary for intensive development in the long run. If so, integration through plan coordination may only be a medium-term solution to problems of the intensive phase. This policy can create an atmosphere wherein "new type" technocrats become more powerful and progressively identify their interests with regional actors, which can spread Soviet penetration making for increased CMEA discipline and aiding the chances of success for a real supranatural body. But, such factors may permanently alienate reformist technocrats, who would have little interest in retaining an administrative-type system, yet who also manage the necessary short-term infusion of Western technology.

This would increase the *likelihood* of domestic dissent, such as the circulation of Charter 77 in Czechoslovakia. If such dissent is accompanied by mass discontent, the continuation of a conservative system could create a powerful impetus for radical demands for change. Mass disenchantment is contingent on meeting popular economic and political demands. Economically, the lack of long-term solutions for innovative questions and continued stress on imbalanced growth may mean that consumerism cannot be satisfied. Eventually, new sacrifices may be called for. Yet, negative popular reaction to the relatively small sacrifices under NEM, which nevertheless provided for overall increased consumption, indicates little mass sufferance. In addition, the decreased national sovereignty inherent in integration, especially under joint planning, challenges the national ethos, partially accommodated by the party elites into their ideology in the inclusion phase. How will this political reconciliation be maintained if integration progresses? The masses could join reformists in opposing the party and its new techniques as foreign agents. Whatever the degree of progress toward regional integration in CMEA, it seems clear that the forms domestic change may take will be cast in a largely conservative, controlled mold.

Notes

1. Robert Nisbet, "Introduction: The Problem of Social Change," in Robert Nisbet, ed., *Social Change* (New York: Harper & Row, 1972), p. 1.

2. Ibid, p. 14.

3. See Chalmers Johnson, "Comparing Communist Nations," in Chalmers Johnson, ed., *Change in Communist Systems* (Stanford, Calif.: Stanford University Press, 1970), pp. 1-32.

4. As Jozsef Bognár has observed, "The Communist parties of the individual countries play an especially important part in formulating new conceptions and tendencies in shaping the public opinion associated with integration," in his "The Socio-Political and Institutional Aspects of Integration" (Paper presented to the Fourth World Congress of the International Economic Association, Budapest, August, 1974), p. 25.

5. In distinguishing between vertical connections—as "a matter of authority and subordination" and horizontal connections—which involve contact of one enterprise with other enterprises . . . [all] having equal rights and standing, Kornai says that "vertical connections are dominant ones . . . [since] the influences which result from direct contacts between enterprises are dwarfed by those which result from indirect contacts." János Kornai, *Overcentralization in Economic Administration* (London: Oxford University Press, 1959), pp. 191-94.

6. Nisbet, "Introduction," pp. 14-16.

7. See Kenneth Jowitt, "Inclusion and Mobilization in European Leninist Regimes," *World Politics* 28 (October 1974), pp. 69-75; Mark Field, "Introduction," in Mark Field, ed., *Social Consequences of Modernization in Communist Societies* (Baltimore, Md.: Johns Hopkins University Press, 1976), pp. 1-18; and Zvi Y. Gitelman, "Power and Authority in Eastern Europe," in Chalmers Johnson,

ed., *Change in Communist Systems*, pp. 235-65.

8. Jowitt, "Inclusion and Mobilization," pp. 69-75.

9. This point is best reflected in Peter C. Ludz, *The Changing Party Elite in East Germany* (Cambridge, Mass.: MIT Press, 1971). and in his *The German Democratic Republic from the Sixties to the Seventies* (Cambridge, Mass.: Center for International Affairs, 1970), pp. 39-41.

10. Radoslav Selucky, *Economic Reforms in Eastern Europe* (New York: Praeger, 1972), pp. 26-39.

11. See Selucky, *Economic Reforms;* and Vladimir V. Kusin, "Comments: Political Aspects" in Zbigniew Fallenbuchl, ed., *Economic Development in Eastern Europe and the Soviet Union*, vol. I (New York: Praeger, 1975), pp. 100-101.

12. Jowitt, "Inclusion and Mobilization," p. 91.

13. Susan Bodenheimer, "Dependency and Imperialism," in K.T. Fann and Donald C. Hodges, eds., *Readings in U.S. Imperialism* (Boston: Porter Sargent, 1971), p. 163. Johan Galtung has explicitly drawn this parallel for international communism on political and military dimensions; see his "A Structural Theory of Imperialism," *Journal of Peace Research* 8 (1971), pp. 94-96.

14. Theotonio Dos Santos, "The Structure of Dependence," in Fann and Hodges, eds., *Readings in U.S. Imperialism*, p. 226.

15. For a discussion of this type of dependence, see James Caporaso, "Methodological Issues in the Measurement of Inequality and Exploitation," in Steven J. Rosen and James R. Kurth, eds., *Testing Theories of Imperialism* (Lexington, Mass.: D.C. Heath, 1974), p. 91.

16. Paul Marer, "The Political Economy of Soviet Relations with Eastern Europe," in Rosen and Kurth, eds., *Testing Theories of Imperialism*, pp. 251-53.

17. Johan Galtung, *The European Community: A Superpower in the Making* (London: George Allen and Unwin Ltd., 1973), pp. 87-89.

18. Marer, "Political Economy," pp. 247-49; Michael Barrett Brown, *The Economics of Imperialism* (Harmondsworth, G.B.: Penguin Books, 1974), p. 299; Jürgen Nötzold, "Limits of East-West Trade," in Stanislav Wasowski, ed., *East-West Trade and the Technology Gap* (New York: Praeger, 1970), pp. 164, 178; and Michael Kaser, "Review Article: Technology and Oil in Comecon's

External Relations, *Journal of Common Market Studies* (March 13, 1975), p. 163.

19. Zbigniew M. Fallenbuchl, "Comecon Integration," *Problems of Communism* (March/April 1973), pp. 30, 32, 36.

20. Catherine Séranne, "Les Situations D'Inégalité au sein du Conseil D'Assistance Economique Mutuelle (COMECON)," *Etudes Internationales* 2 (1971), p. 275; and Marer, "Political Economy," p. 253.

21. J.M.P. van Brabant, *Essays on Planning, Trade and Integration in Eastern Europe* (Rotterdam: Rotterdam University Press, 1974), pp. 273-80.

22. Marer, "Political Economy," p. 250.

23. Robert W. Dean, *West German Trade with the East: The Political Dimension* (New York: Praeger, 1974), pp. 236-38. See also John P. Hardt, "Imperatives of Economic Reform," this volume.

24. Brabant, *Essays on Planning*, p.163.

25. F. Pindak, "Comecon's Programme of 'Socialist Economic Integration,'" *Jahrbuch der Wirtschaft Osteuropas* 5 (1973), pp. 435, 436.

26. A. Axline, "Integration, Development and Dependence: The Politics of Regionalism in the Third World" (Paper presented to the Caribbean Studies Association, St. Lucia, West Indies, Jan. 1976), p. 12; Roger Hanson, "Regional Integration: Reflections on a Decade of Theoretical Efforts," *World Politics* 21 (1969), pp. 255-60.

27. M. Simai, "The Two Strategies of Integration and East-West Relations," mimeographed (Budapest: Karl Marx University, 1974), pp. 13, 18, 19.

28. Radoslav Selucky, "Reform Movement in Eastern Europe and Socialist Economic Integration" (Paper presented to 5th National Convention AAASS, Dallas, Texas, March 15-18, 1972), p. 4.

29. Selucky, "Reform Movement in Eastern Europe," p. 21; Fallenbuchl, "Comecon Integration," p. 39.

30. P. Alampiev, O. Bogomolov, and Y. Shiryaev, *A New Approach to Economic Integration* (Moscow: Progress Publishers, 1974), pp. 78, 79.

31. Bennett Kovrig, *The Hungarian People's Republic* (Baltimore, Md.: Johns Hopkins University Press, 1970), pp. 20-27.

32. William F. Robinson, *The Pattern of Reform in Hungary: A Political, Economic and Cultural Analysis* (New York: Praeger, 1973), pp. 390-95.

33. For instance, see Rezsö Nyers, *Gazdaságpolitikank és a Gazdasági Mechanizmus Reformja* (Budapest: Kossuth Könyvkiado, 1968), pp. 114-31 (Speech originally published in 1965); György Ránki, *Magyarország Gazdasága Az Elso Három-Éves Terv Idöszakban* (Budapest: Közgazdasagi es Jogi Könyvkiado, 1963); and Ivan T. Berend, *Gazdaságpolitika Az Elso Öteves Terv Miginditásákor* (Budapest: Közgazdasagi es Jogi Könyvkiado, 1964).

34. Harry G. Shaffer, "Progress in Hungary," *Problems of Communism* 19 (January-February 1970), p. 50.

35. See Ivan Berend, "The Historical Background of the Recent Economic Reforms in East Europe: The Hungarian Experiences," *East European Quarterly* 2 (September 1969); and Selucky, *Economic Reforms*, pp. 3-51, 135-48; Arpad Abonyi, *Hungary's New Economic Mechanism within a Regional Framework of Comecon Integration, 1968-1971*, M.A. thesis, School of International Affairs (Ottawa: Carleton University, 1971), pp. 88-127.

36. Jozsef Bognár, "Introduction," *Handbook of Hungarian Foreign Trade* (Budapest: Corvina, 1972), p. 13.

37. Istvan Hetényi, "National Economic Planning in the New System of Economic Control and Management," in Istvan Friss, ed., *Reform of the New Economic Mechanism in Hungary* (Budapest: Kossuth, 1972), p. 43.

38. Géza P. Lauter, *The Manager and Economic Reform in Hungary* (New York: Praeger, 1972), p. 42; and János Lászlo, "Népgazdasági Tervezés és Gazdasági Szabályok, *Valoság* 2 (1973), pp. 56-64.

39. Imre Vajda, "Foreign Trade and Economic Reform in the New Technical Age," *Hungarian Survey* 1 (1967), pp. 19-35 and elsewhere.

40. Jenö Wilcsek, "Functions of State-Owned Enterprises," in Friss, *Reform of the Economic Mechanism*, pp. 210-13; and Lauter, *The Manager*, pp. 55-56; and Béla Szulyok, "Major Financial Regulators in the New System of Economic Control and Management," in Friss, *Reform of the Economic Mechanism*, pp. 167-78.

41. Szulyok, "Major Financial Regulators," pp. 178-80.

42. Béla Csikos-Nagy, "The New Hungarian Price System," in Friss, *Reform of the Economic Mechanism*, pp. 137-39.

43. S. Balazsy, "Foreign Trade and the Reform of the New Economic Management," *Acta Oeconomica* 7 (1966), p. 315.

44. Balazsy, "Foreign Trade," pp. 317, 323; and Lauter, *The Manager*, p. 57.

45. Hungarian trade dependence is demonstrated in the set of figures in Tables 1 and 2.

Table 1.   Hungary's Foreign Trade with the Soviet Union and other East European members of CMEA, 1967–1971 (value in millions of current dollars percentage increase from previous year and percentage share)

	Value in 1971	Percentage Increase			Percentage Share	
		1967–1971	1970	1971	1967	1971
EXPORTS						
Soviet Union	873	7.3	11.2	7.9	36.1	34.9
Other East European						
countries	745	8.8	1.2	20.6	28.8	29.8
Total, all countries	2500	8.0	11.2	7.9	100.0	100.0
IMPORTS						
Soviet Union	1021	11.5	16.3	23.1	33.3	34.1
Other East European						
countries	868	9.9	36.9	20.9	30.5	29.0
Total, all countries	2990	11.0	30.0	19.3	100.0	100.0

Source: United Nations Economic Bulletin for Europe 23, no. 1 (New York, 1971):27.

Table 2.   Hungarian Imports of Essential Raw Materials from the Soviet Union in 1969 and 1972 (as a percentage of total imports)

	1969	1972	Percentage Change
Coking Coal	65.5	54.2	–11.3
Petroleum	79.0	99.0	+20
Iron Ore	79.5	99.6	+20.1

Sources: 1969 figures from "Essai d'inventaire économique des pays de l'Est," *Travaux et recherches,* no. 19 (1969), p. 168; 1972 figures computed from *Külkeresdelmi Statisztikai Évkonyv* (Budapest: Kosponti Statisztikai Hivatal, 1973), pp. 76, 79.

46. Information obtained through interviews conducted with economists and planners in Hungary, spring 1974.

47. One such informal agreement resulted from a luncheon at Moscow airport between Lajos Fehér, the Politburo member responsible for agricultural policy, and his Soviet counterpart, while the Hungarian was on a stopover on his way to Mongolia. The agreement called for a substantial increase in the delivery of certain agricultural products to the Soviet Union. Hungarian managers found themselves hard strapped to meet this additional commitment

since it was undertaken without their prior knowledge and didn't figure in their output for the production year. So the National Planning Office had to reshuffle the manager's priorities and issue a new plan letting them know new production targets.

48. Ferenc Kozma, "Some Theoretical Problems Regarding Socialist Integration and the Levelling of Economic Development," *Trends in World Economy*, no. 6 (Budapest: Hungarian Scientific Council for World Economy, 1971), pp. 37-52; and Sándor Ausch, "Plan, Market and Socialist Integration," in Tibor Kiss, ed., *The Market of Socialist Economic Integration* (Budapest: Akademiai Kiado, 1973), pp. 63-77.

49. Henry Wilcox Schaefer, *Comecon and the Politics of Integration* (New York: Praeger, 1972), pp. 6, 7.

50. Ibid. Recognition of this problem also helped spur reforms in the countries suffering most from resource scarcities, i.e., the GDR, Czechoslovakia, and Hungary.

51. Tibor Kiss, *Nemzetközi Munka megösztás és Magyarország Gazdasági Növekedése* (Budapest: Kossuth, 1969), pp. 192, 202-204.

52. The Hungarian position was articulated in Antal Ápro, *A KGST-országok gasdasági együtmüködése és a magyar népgazdaság* (Budapest: Kossuth, 1968); Sándor Ausch, *Theory and Practice of CMEA Cooperation* (Budapest: Akademiai Kiado, 1972), originally published in Hungarian in 1969; Kiss, *Nemzetközi*; Rezsö Nyers, *A szocialista gazdasági integracio elvi és gyakorlati kérdései* (Budapest: Kossuth, 1969); T. Földi and T. Kiss, eds., *Socialist World Market Prices* (Budapest: Akademiai Kiado, 1969); Tibor Kiss, "A KGST-országok nemzeti piacainak integracioja," *Közgazdasági Szemle* (May 1970), pp. 525-38; and Tibor Kiss, *The Market of Socialist Economic Integration* (Budapest: Akademiai Kiado, 1973).

53. Antal Ápro, "A Nemzeti és nemzetközi érdeke osszefonodása," *Társadalmi Szemle* 23 (December 1968), pp. 8, 10.

54. Rezsö Nyers, "A szocialista gazdasági integracio problémája," *Külkeresdelem*, no. 2 (February 1969), pp. 42, 43.

55. Kiss, *Nemzetközi*, pp. 132, 133, and 140-47.

56. Dorothy Miller and Harry G. Trend, "Economic Reforms in East Germany," *Problems of Communism* 15 (March - April 1966), p. 32; Schaefer, *Comecon*, pp. 74, 75; and Robinson, *Pattern of Reform*, pp. 190-91.

57. Information obtained through interviews conducted in Hungary, spring 1974. In addition see Stephen C. Stolte, "Comecon on the Threshold of the Seventies," *Institute for the USSR Bulletin* 17 (July 1970), pp. 21-23.

58. Schaefer, *Comecon*, p. 74, 75; and A. Lyutov, "Economic

Integration and the Socialist International Market," in T. Kiss, *The Market*, p. 55.

59. Robinson, *Pattern of Reform*, pp. 194, 195.

60. See Fallenbuchl, "Comecon Integration," p. 36, 37; and Schaefer, *Comecon*.

61. Schaefer, *Comecon*; and Sándor Ausch, "Plan, Market and Socialist Integration," in T. Kiss, ed., *The Market*, pp. 63-76.

62. This conference was edited in book form; see T. Kiss, ed., *The Market*.

63. See *The Comprehensive Programme for the Futher Extension and Improvement of Cooperation and Development of Social and Economic Integration by the CMEA Member Countries* (Moscow: Progress Publishers, 1971).

64. Pindak, "Comecon's Programme," pp. 451-52.

65. This relies on available information on the decision-making apparatuses in IEAs; see Ivan J. Sylvain, "A Typology of Cooperative Ventures in the CMEA" (Paper presented to annual meeting of Canadian Association of Slavists, May 30–June 2, 1976), pp. 11, 19-22.

66. Peter Marsh, "The Integration Process in Eastern Europe: 1968 to 1975," *Journal of Common Market Studies* 14 (June 1976), pp. 330-32, among many other studies stressing this point.

67. Alampiev, et al., *A New Approach to Economic Integration*, pp. 81-88.

68. See David Granick, "Hungarian Economic Reforms," *World Politics* 25 (April 1973), pp. 415-29; Marie Lavigne, "Economic Reforms: Ten Years After," pp. 44-46, 54-57, and Eugene Zaleski, "Comments: Economic Aspects," pp. 108-110, both in Fallenbuchl, *Economic Development*; and Charles Gati, "The Kádár Mystique," *Problems of Communism* 23 (May-June 1974), pp. 23-35.

69. Gati, "Kádár Mystique," p. 30.

70. Andrzej Korbonski, "Détente and East-West Trade, and the Future of Economic Integration in Eastern Europe," *World Politics* 28 (July 1976), pp. 587-88; and Marsh, "Integration Process," pp. 322-38.

71. Marsh, "Integration Process," p. 332.

72. Harry Trend, "Comecon's Organization Structure," *Radio Free Europe Research*, RAD Background Report 38, Eastern Europe (7 October 1975), p. 7.

73. Marsh, "Integration Process," p. 332.

74. Roger Kanet, "East-West Trade and the Limits of Western Influence," in Charles Gati, ed., *The International Politics of Eastern*

Europe (New York: Praeger, 1976), pp. 208, 209.

75. Marsh, "Integration Process," pp. 311-35.

76. Teresa Rakowska-Harmstone, "Socialist Internationalism, Pt. 1," *Survey* 22 (winter 1976), pp. 38-54.

77. See *Radio Free Europe Research*, Hungarian Situation Report (Sitrep) 9 (April 1972), pp. 16-17; and Robinson, *Pattern of Reform*, p. 193.

78. *Radio Free Europe Research*, Hungarian Sitrep 14 (23 March 1973), p. 15.

79. Barnabas Buky, "Hungary's NEM on a Treadmill," *Problems of Communism* 21 (September-October 1971), p. 37.

80. For Hungarian complaints, see K. Botos in Harry Trend, ed., "New Comecon Joint Investments—But Some Old Problems Remain," *Radio Free Europe Research*, RAD Background Report 46, Eastern Europe (12 March 1976), p. 6.

81. Paul Marer, "Has Eastern Europe Become a Liability to the Soviet Union (III)—The Economic Aspect," in Gati, *International Politics*, pp. 72, 73, 75, 81.

82. *Radio Free Europe Research*, Hungarian Sitreps 8 (25 February 1975), pp. 4-7; 6 (18 February 1976), pp. 4-6.

83. See *Radio Free Europe Research*, Hungarian Sitrep 46 (4 November 1975), pp. 4, 5.

84. Marie Lavigne, "Economic Reforms in Eastern Europe: Ten Years After," in Fallenbuchl, *Economic Development*, pp. 45, 46.

85. *Radio Free Europe Research*, Hungarian Sitreps 23 (3 July 1973), p. 6, 8; and 20 June 1974.

86. *Radio Free Europe Research*, Hungarian Sitrep 17 (9 April 1975), passim., especially pp. 8, 9.

87. See *Radio Free Europe Research*, Hungarian Sitreps 30 (8 July 1975), pp. 11-16; 35 (19 August 1975), pp. 2, 3; and 37 (2 Setember 1975), pp. 1-3.

88. *See Radio Free Europe Research*, Hungarian Sitreps 42 (7 October 1975), pp. 2-4; 43 (14 October 1974), pp. 2-4; 46 (4 November 1975), passim; 44 (22 October 1975), passim; 45 (29 October 1975), passim. Morra, in Bornstein.

89. Robinson, *Pattern of Reform*; and *Radio Free Europe Research*, Hungarian Sitreps 17 (9 April 1975), pp. 8, 9; 35 (19 August 1975), pp. 2, 3.

90. *Radio Free Europe Research*, Hungarian Sitrep 23 (20 May 1975), pp. 4, 5.

91. Compare the only partial resurrection of reformer Mátyás

Timár, and the demotion of Imre Dimény, closely associated with Fehér, to the promotion of technocrats drawn from planning institutions and heavy industry, such as István Huszár, Gyula Szeker, and Pál Romany. Certain *apparatchiks*, such as Tividár Nemeslaki and Ferenc Havasi, were also promoted at this time. *Radio Free Europe Research*, Hungarian Sitrep 30 (8 July 1975), pp. 6-8.

6
Participation, Change, and Stability: Yugoslavia in Comparative Perspective

Gary K. Bertsch

The nature and extent of sociopolitical change in postwar Yugoslavia, particularly as it relates to the question of popular participation and party rule, is a question of considerable concern to observers of Communist state affairs. After briefly exploring the issues of popular participation and change in Eastern Europe and the Soviet Union, this chapter examines the nature and extent of varous aspects of change in the Yugoslav system. Unlike the leaders of most Communist party systems, the Yugoslavs have shown a willingness to implement political changes to keep abreast of their changing society. Showing less conservatism than their Soviet and East European counterparts, the Yugoslavs have experimented with reforms that have made Yugoslavia the most innovative of all Communist systems.

Popular Participation and Political Change in the Soviet Union and Eastern Europe

Firmly rooted in orthodox Marxist-Leninist thought is the idea that citizen involvement and popular participation are the most reliable guards against the excesses of bureaucratism and statism. While early Marxist philosophers held rather utopian expectations regarding the likelihood of self-administration under socialism in the realm of sociopolitical affairs, Soviet practice in the first Marxist-Leninist state soon quashed such illusory visions. Although Lenin's early concept of government was built upon the expectation of mass citizen participation, as noted in the slogan "every cook a Commissar" and in his statement that "under socialism all will administer,"[1] he was soon willing to admit his own misgivings and dismiss his earlier conception as a "fairy tale."[2]

As Lenin increasingly came to grips with the realities confronting Russia's difficult situation, he and the other high party officials wrested greater and greater power from the more direct organs of citizen administration and control. His justification for the assumption of such power was based upon the perceived administrative inadequacies of the masses. "These elements are not sufficiently educated," he noted. "They would like to build a better apparat for us, but they do not know how. They cannot build one. They have not yet acquired the culture for this; and it is the culture that is required."[3] At the time Lenin's justification might have appeared quite feasible, for it would not seem unreasonable to have a highly centralized, well-organized elite assume predominant control during the initial stages of postrevolutionary consolidation, modernization, and system-building. Then, as the broader populace became "sufficiently educated" and developed "the culture that is required," one might expect the regime to allocate increasing levels of power and afford more opportunities for participation in the interests of promoting citizen involvement and mass control.

For the most part, however, political trends in the areas of popular participation and party control characterizing the next fifty years of Soviet development showed little movement in this direction. Although some tentative steps were taken— for example, Stalin's "move to the left" at the Fifteenth Party Congress and Khrushchev's populist formula, expressed in the late 1950's and more fully articulated in the 1961 Party Program—the overall pattern was to deny citizens access to any genuine aspect of control that should have accompanied their educational and cultural gains.[4] The guiding principle at work, then, seemed to be based upon political motives quite unrelated to the sophistication of the masses. The motives of the leaders defining this policy seemed to suggest that the optimal development of Soviet society could be coordinated and accomplished most effectively by the CPSU, or as some say, "from above." So long as elites were successful in mobilizing the masses to carry out the wishes of the planners, there was little reason or value accorded the encouragement of participation that might prove to interfere with the concerted drive originating at the top of the party hierarchy.[5]

What has evolved, according to the views of many close observers of Communist party states, is a growing gap between the capabilities of the masses and the political forms or institutions of the state. Those political forms that have been developed are described most often as hollow, "pseudo-type" institutions that undermine the real meaning of genuine participatory democracy.[6] What may result is a population that is "more advanced" than the political institutions of the state, or in other words a citizenry that has "outgrown" the political forms designed for its use. This lack of correspondence or synchronization between the attributes of the populace and those of the political system, as well as the growing disparity between what the individual or the collective is told to exist and what exists in fact, suggests rather serious implications concerning the long-run stability of the system.[7] To this issue we will turn after briefly considering the conservative change process governing Soviet and East European development.

Political Change and Communist Development: System Maintenance or System Persistence?

Why has the process of political change in most of the Marxist-Leninist states of Eastern Europe and the Soviet Union been marked by a relative failure in the evolution of genuine participatory forms? After observing the change process and its general undemocratic content in these states, one leading observer explains the pattern as a consequence of an essentially conservative developmental strategy. In that regard, Gitelman contends that the foremost objective governing the change strategy of the one-party Communist regimes has been that of *system maintenance*[8]—what David Easton refers to as a goal to salvage "the existing pattern of relationships" and to direct continuing "attention to their preservation."[9] This is, of course, a closed strategy that resists liberal-type changes even when forces emanating from the environment may recommend appropriate political innovations. Easton suggests that a strategy more appropriate to all political systems would be that of *system persistence*.[10] In this regard, he argues that in order to persist (i.e., continue to allocate values) a system must be less concerned with maintaining the status quo and more concerned with changing and adapting itself to fluctuating circumstances (an idea related to the logic of systems analysis, which posits that change in one aspect of a social system necessitates change in another). According to Easton, "Persistence signalizes the importance of considering, not any particular structure or pattern, but rather the very life processes of systems themselves."[11] Systems persistence, therefore, may require extensive or radical alterations to certain aspects of the inner workings of the political system itself. A question of concern to us here is the apparent unwillingness or inability of the Soviet and East European Communist states to make these alterations as changes occur within their environment, and in particular, within their citizenry.

Gitelman's position as regards the East European scene is that

> since the mid-1950's the European Communist systems seem to have become very concerned with system maintenance and incapable of evolving strategies and tactics for the longer-range purpose of system persistence. This is due to the arrestation of the Soviet system at the Leninist-Stalinist stage of development,

and its insistence that other East European systems adhere to its pattern. By and large, East European Communist systems have failed to evolve effective political institutions and behavioral patterns for the post-mobilization era of their development. This failure is due to ideological and structural constraints which are maintained by leadership behavior patterns.[12]

In other words, Gitelman maintains that Soviet conservatism is responsible for arresting the normal development of citizen involvement thus interfering with system synchronization. The supporting rationale is that although rather extensive alterations have taken place with the postmobilization society, rather limited changes have been made in the political realm. In Gitelman's estimation, the consequence is a state of atrophy in the process of political development, and consequently, political decay rather than political growth.[13]

Close examination of the change patterns exhibited in Eastern Europe and the Soviet Union, and all that has been written about them, shows some policies suggesting system persistence. However, of critical importance is that if these policy changes were indeed legitimate attempts to accommodate the various stresses emanating from changes in the society, they were still basically conservative in nature and untrusting of the essentially liberal values of genuine political participation and bona fide self-management of social, economic, and cultural affairs.[14] For the most part, this liberalization (de-Stalinization) was represented by what might be referred to as pseudoparticipation in work and social organizations of limited credibility as organs of genuine participation and representation.

The question is whether these conservative attempts at system persistence in the East European countries[15] were to be preferred in terms of the system's own self-interests over more liberal policies guaranteeing higher levels of participation. Specifically, has the conservative political change evidenced in Eastern Europe and the Soviet Union over the last quarter decade been more or less satisfactory, for example, than the more liberal change that has occurred in Yugoslavia? Easton appears to assist in addressing this question when he speaks of the *type* of political change and "successful adaptation." According to Easton, change is satisfactory and successful so long as the adaptation ensures that the political system persists.[16] According to Easton's criterion, political change and adaptation among East European systems has been successful, at least over the short run, just because of their apparent stability and persistence. But as has been noted elsewhere,[17] almost all systems as defined by Easton have been persisting through centuries, and the only time they cease to persist is when the effective allocation of values disappears due to "some natural disaster such as earthquake or epidemic, or when the society has failed to reproduce itself biologically."[18]

If such be the case, and a careful reading of Easton suggests that it is, how do we distinguish between satisfactory and unsatisfactory, or beneficial and harmful political change? In that regard, the following criteria for evaluating political change are suggested. First, do the policies representing political changes within the system correspond with the values upon which the state is based? In this instance, is there a gap between the Marxist-Leninist value of mass involvement and the policies adopted by the particular regime? Second, do the political changes instituted by the regime correspond with the capabilities of the masses? If the answers to these two questions are in the affirmative, then we might evaluate the political change as satisfactory. If one or the other is answered negatively, we might conclude the obverse. According to observations of many Western and non-Western scholars alike, the changes taking place in Eastern Europe and the Soviet Union would be termed unsatisfactory. By their judgments, present policies have often failed to correspond with the proclaimed values of the state ideology, and at the same time, have lacked any real correspondence to the capabilities of the masses.

Popular Participation and Communist Development: Civil Strife or Socialist Tranquility?

In an effort to draw some meaning from participation and political change in Communist party states as they relate to societal stability, it is interesting to view the relationship in light of recent theoretical and empirical studies. Although studies and theories abound, a perspective widely accepted among Western social scientists is that internal political instability in the form of civil conflict is likely to result from a condition known as relative deprivation.[19] Defined as a psychological condition, this variable denotes an individual or collective's perception of the discrepancy between their own value expectations and their environment's value capabilities. Value expectations are defined as the conditions of life to which people believe they are entitled, and value capabilities refer to what people are in fact capable of attaining given the realities of the environment. Gurr divides the values most relevant to a theory of relative deprivation into three types: welfare values, power values, and interpersonal values.[20] It is the second category that we are concerned with in this analysis. Gurr defines it in the following manner:

> Power values are those that determine the extent to which men can influence the actions of others and avoid unwanted interference by others in their own actions. Power values especially salient for political violence include the desire to participate in collective decision-making—to vote, to take part in political competition, to become a member of the political elite—and the related desires for self-determination and security, for example freedom from oppressive political regulation or from disorder.[21]

Taking this basic political value as applied to the idea of value expectations and capabilities, the theory of relative deprivation posits that the greater the disparity between expectations and

Figure 1. Variables Influencing Civil Strife

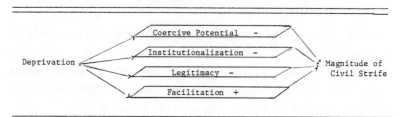

Deprivation → Coercive Potential −
Institutionalization −
Legitimacy −
Facilitation + → Magnitude of Civil Strife

Adapted from Gurr, "A Causal Model," p. 219.

capabilities, the more likely the incidence of civil strife.[22]

The basic theory has been refined to explain the magnitude of civil strife by incorporating four additional variables into the model—coercive potential, institutionalization, facilitation, and legitimacy.[23] Although Gurr cautions that the relationship between the variables and the magnitude of civil strife are not necessarily linear ones, the basic hypothesis is as follows: the higher the level of coercive potential on the part of the regime, institutionalization of associational structures, and legitimacy of the regime, and the lower the factors facilitating civil strife, the lower the magnitude of civil strife within any deprivation setting (see Figure 1).

Although it is of course risky to discuss hypothetically a psychological variable such as this one, it does not seem unfair to speculate about the potential for relative deprivation and societal instability in Eastern Europe and the Soviet Union; that is, do the masses feel deprived in respect to the power they wield in the political system? If so, is this sense of deprivation likely to result in civil disorder?

In respect to these questions, any response covering all of the peoples and groups in the Soviet Union and Eastern Europe will of course represent a gross oversimplification. Yet a possible answer to the first would be that, due to historical realities (e.g., the absence of a strong democratic tradition) and the contemporary characteristics of the masses (e.g., the apolitical feelings of the broad majority), the sense of deprivation is not nearly so high as the casual observer might suspect. Secondly, even if the sense of relative deprivation and the potential for civil disorder were high, the likelihood for societal instability in Eastern Europe and the Soviet Union would be low. The four forces in Figure 1 suggest why. In the countries under investigation, the sociopolitical context is designed to militate against an expression of collective violence and societal instability, as the coercive potential of the state over the society, or any part thereof, is strong enough to deter any rebellion. Next, the high level of associational structures in terms of party, work, and social organizations broaden the alternative ways for an individual to gain value satisfaction and thereby displace (or diffuse) the frustration that might normally be expressed through violent or revolutionary behaviors. Thirdly, the regimes' success in gaining the compliance and support of the populace tends to diffuse or soften the frustration resulting from the relative deprivation. Lastly, the control, or at least discouragement, of social and structural elements (e.g., dissident movements) deters the coalescence of growing frustration into collective rebellion or violence. All these factors are likely to defuse the destablizing force of relative deprivation that might be present among the populations of Communist party states.

At the same time, however, what we know about the Soviet and East European peoples' feelings toward their lack of power would suggest that a certain amount of tension exists and that it is likely to grow in the future. This psychological state may lie dormant over a number of years, and then quickly grow and erupt into political violence under a certain set of conditions. Illustrative, perhaps, is the Hungarian rebellion of 1956, and the Polish uprisings of the 1970s, which resulted when the coercive potential of the state was temporarily relaxed together with the coalescence of collective frustration. While bearing in mind the hypothetical situations and practical experiences of other East European systems, we move on to a consideration of the Yugoslav experience.

Yugoslav Developments: From Centralized to Self-Managing Socialism

One of the most interesting characteristics of the Yugoslav leaders is what Dennison Rusinov has referred to as their "inexhaustible willingness to experiment." In broad terms, the Yugoslavs have encouraged in some cases, and permitted in others, changes that have taken their system rather far away from the Soviet-type system. It would be difficult to argue, under any circumstances, that the Yugoslav system has been "arrested at the Leninist-Stalinist stage of development."

After an initial period (1947-52) of centralized management and administration, the Yugoslavs began experimenting with a variety of self-administrative forms.[24] The first came with the institution of workers' self-management in the form of workers' councils in the early 1950s,[25] and the second came with the communal system of self-government in 1955.[26] The Yugoslav constitution guarantees every work collective the rights of self-management and sets down the obligations of the working people to the society.[27] In exercising the rights and obligations of self-management, the work groups elect a variety of decison-making bodies that determine the right of direct and indirect participation in the affairs of the work organization. Although there has been considerable controversy over who is qualified and who is ultimately responsible for making decisions within the enterprise, there does appear to be widespread commitment to involving as much worker participation as "qualifications" and "expertise" permit;[28] that is, while there is widespread agreement on the value of the broader concept of worker self-management, controversy arises when getting down to the more specific questions of "who decides" on the basis of "what information."[29] Overall, however, the content and scope of the self-administrative responsibilities are laid down by the 1974 constitution and the 1976 Law on Associated Labor.

The second aspect of local participation and self-government in Yugoslavia was instituted within the local territorial community in the form of the communal system of government. The Yugoslav constitution and the Program of the League of Communists guarantee the status of the commune as a self-managing community organized as a sociopolitical form to manage common local affairs. The nature of such affairs is broad and includes functions and responsibilities in political, social, economic, cultural, and educational realms. In each realm, the commune and the decision-making bodies therein are concerned with the fundamental task of reconciling general and individual interests within the territorial community. Although research has suggested that some communes have been far more active and effective than others, Yugoslav leaders appear genuinely committed to making the commune an increasingly meaningful institution of self-government. In that regard, Hunnius notes that "the commune is seen by Yugoslav theoreticians as the fundamental cell of a future socialist society."[30]

In light of the almost voluminous research—both Yugoslav and non-Yugoslav—on the role and nature of worker self-management and the communal system of self-government in Yugoslav society, there is good reason to conclude that participatory democracy in the country is thriving and growing stronger. The Yugoslavs now see themselves in the third administrative phase, having moved beyond the centralized period of 1947-52, then through the experimentation of 1953-64, and finally into a period of institutionalization and consolidation that has no peer in the Communist world.

Although some observers believed that the internal difficulties experienced by Yugoslavia in the early 1970's might cause the leaders to reconsider their rapid movement toward self-managing socialism, this has not been the case. While the leaders did move to reassert the leading role of the League of

Communists of Yugoslavia (LCY) and encourage more centralized and long-term planning, they also moved to strengthen and expand the self-management system. The 1974 constitution and the more recent Law on Associated Labor have moved the system structurally and ideologically closer to a self-managing socialist system. At a meeting of the Presidency of the Central Committee of the LCY in June of 1977, the country's chief ideologist and often considered second in command, Edvard Kardelj, reemphasized the pluralism of self-management interests that must "find expression within the framework of democratic self-management decision-making as directly and freely as possible." After ten years of close observation and research on the self-management system, I am prepared to say that Kardelj is perfectly serious, means what he says, and has every intention of seeing democratic decision making carried out. This fundamental objective, however, comes into conflict with the traditional Communist state characteristic of party rule.[31]

Political Change and the Role of the LCY

Yugoslav elites have been continually confronted since the early years of the self-management movement with the question of the proper type and role of the party under the rapidly changing conditions of Yugoslav socialism. What kind of party is best suited to the Yugoslav situation? And, can the party evolve in a fashion that keeps pace with other rapid changes in the Yugoslav sociopolitical setting?

Tito and the Yugoslav leaders began their careers in governing the new socialist state by utilizing a party designed according to the Soviet mold. The highly centralized, active Communist party of Yugoslavia played a leading Leninist role in the initial administrative period. With the subsequent movement toward self-managing socialism, with its unavoidable pluralization within work organizations and federation, the centralized party role came into question. Would the increasing power of the enterprises, communes, republics, and provinces mean a decline of power on the part of the party? Obviously it would, and the 1950s and 1960s saw a slow but steady decline of the party's power. This period was marked by symbolic changes, such as new nomenclature for the Communist party (after 1952, the League of Communists), and real changes where the republic and provincial party levels took on increasing power, leading many observers to speak of the "federalization of the party." During this period, leaders spoke of "divorcing the party from power,"[32] and efforts were made to promote the participation of governmental, economic, and sociopolitical organs to take a more meaningful role in the decision-making process, often at the expense of the party. While some might contend that this process resulted only after careful planning and synoptic decision making within the party itself, most now contend that it was the result of "ideological drift" during which the party was frantically searching for its proper role.[33]

The drift and search were temporarily ended in the early 1970s when Tito and the party leaders decided to intervene to quell the threatening nationalist tendencies in Croatia, in particular, but elsewhere as well, and to end the trend toward excessive technocratism and ideological pluralism. This was perhaps the most dangerous challenge that the Communists had yet incurred in their new socialist state, and they responded with a reassertion of party power, prompting some observers to comment about a return to Leninism.[34] The 1974 constitution and Tenth Congress of the LCY that followed this unsettling period reaffirmed that "we Communists are in control of this country,"[35] and that the LCY was the ultimate organ of power and responsibility.

The period between the Tenth Congress (1974) and the Eleventh Congress (1978) saw a certain softening of the Leninist position and a realization that strict, centralized party rule and self-managing socialism were, at least in part, a contradiction. During this period, many LCY spokespersons, most prominently Edvard Kardelj, observed that the LCY's power was not absolute and that they should use caution in their leadership roles within the self-managing system. According to Kardelj in 1977, a prevalent failing of the party was an excess and misuse of power and illegitimate intervention in the self-manage-ment process. Kardelj repeatedly admonished the party and noted that it would often need to retreat and leave decison making to other responsible decision-making bodies. On the eve of the Eleventh Congress of the LCY in June of 1978, the party still grappled with the need and its inevitable desire to play its protective role of control and centralization without impeding democratic decision making within a dynamic and changing society. The party, in other words, is still "in search of its role."

In retrospect, it is apparent that the sociopolitical change characterizing the self-management movement has had a major impact upon the LCY. Whether the change caused alterations in the party's nature and roles, or the evolving party brought about the changes, or whether they are too closely intertwined to distinguish cause and effect is im-material here. That there has been a severe challenge to party discipline and unity is important, and the resulting breakdown has clearly distinguished the LCY from its CPSU counterpart as well as other ruling Communist parties in the world today. The breakdown in party discipline and the decentralization of power, while restored to a considerable extent in the early 1970s, were of course necessary if there was to be any meaning-ful movement toward a genuine participatory democracy. At the same time, this major change away from the orthodox Leninist party, along with the emergence of the republic and provincial party organizations as powerful actors, has resulted in a party without a clear political center. What this fact might mean in the post-Tito era is a question worthy of some consideration.

The role of the LCY in 1978 and the constitutional

preparations made for Tito's passing suggest once again that Yugoslavia has changed a good deal over the years. The party/governmental structure of power finds capable young party activists in the highest bodies of the LCY, most notably the Executive Committee of the LCY, and aging but respected Tito associates in the top governmental organs, in particular the nine-member State Presidency. This rivalry of leading party and governmental bodies, together with the presence of the federal bureaucracy, military, and active regional leaders, suggests that decentralized leadership will obtain control in the post-Tito period. Given the present constellation and structure of power, the LCY is unlikely to return to a dominant Leninist role. Whether a decentralized LCY, lacking the discipline of counterpart parties like the CPSU, will be capable of integrating the country in the post-Tito period is problematical at best.

Political Culture and Political Change in Yugoslavia

Survey research in Yugoslavia has indicated that the beliefs and opinions of the Yugoslav peoples have undergone considerable change over the last two decades.[36] This changing political culture (or cultures, to express more accurately the heterogeneous, multiethnic Yugoslav setting) has been both a cause and a consequence of the move towards self-managing socialism and more decentralized party rule. The open borders and high level of international travel of the population, the more liberal system of political socialization and comparatively low use of ideological education and indoctrination have had a major impact upon the populace. The attitudes and values of the people are changing; they are becoming more modern, more participatory, and less authoritarian. These changes in political culture, in turn, are influencing the political realm, where leaders must contend with the increasingly participant political culture of the 1970s rather than the parochial, subject culture of the 1950s. Even the most casual observer of Yugoslav schools, factories, and social organizations will recognize a participatory ethic much less evident in counterpart institutions in other European Communist states.

Yet, the task of building a fully developed self-managing culture is not nearly complete. The conflict between authoritarian and democratic value systems is still expressed in all walks of Yugoslav life. Schools are often scenes of explosive struggles between traditionalists and those of less hierarchial persuasions. Yugoslav enterprises continue to show considerable value differences and conflicts between workers and management, between factories, groups, and individuals.[37] Although the hope of a homogeneous political culture reflecting the constitutional ideals of Yugoslav self-management is of course an ideal, there is still considerable need and room for progress in moving the society closer to the constitutional principles.

If political and social change are to take place in a healthy partnership, it is important that they advance together. A review of the Yugoslav political socialization strategy, and educational policy in general, suggests that considerable care is being taken to keep the population abreast of changes and advancements in the political structure.[38] It is too early to judge the success of the strategy, but Yugoslav citizens are being groomed with the skills and values of self-management from the earliest elementary grades through the years of advanced adulthood. The consequence, in my estimation, is an evolving democratic culture much different from its presocialist predecessor. To a greater extent than anytime in Yugoslav history, more people are speaking out, actively involving themselves in everyday social, political, and economic affairs, and showing the early potential of participant political culture.

Ethnicity, as reflected in Yugoslav political culture, is also an important cause and consequence of the broader process of political change. During the national liberation, and even more so in the postwar administrative period, Tito and the party leaders recognized the need to provide the different ethnic groups with both cultural autonomy and decision-making power.[39] Unlike their Soviet counterparts, whose federal structure they copied, the Yugoslav regime moved to establish a true federation in which the ethnic and national groups would be given meaningful parts. This ethnic factor was a very strong force in bringing about the decentralized form of self-managing socialism the Yugoslavs follow today.

Paradoxically, while multiethnicity has encouraged political change in Yugoslavia, it has also limited it. Although the leaders were perceptive in recognizing that a Soviet-style, centralized system would not work well in Yugoslavia, and therefore moved toward a genuine federation (which has recently bordered on a confederation), they realized that to move too far in the direction of decentralization and Western democratic rule could tear the country apart. There is some reason to believe that the leadership wanted very much to go further with its democratization movement of the 1960s and encourage the full pluralization of political and economic life. However, as events unfolded in the late 1960s, democratization resulted in increasing regionalism and an escalation of national tensions, causing the leaders to intervene and stop the process.[40] In other words, the ethnic forces of the country were pushing the system toward a Western-type political conflict where regional parties (the League of Communists of Croatia, for example) were the main aggregators of political and economic interests. This became a very explosive situation, threatening the very unity of the country. Tito's purging of the more nationalistic regional leaders, his reassertion of central LCY control, and the hardening ideological line were seen as rather significant steps backward on what many observers had viewed as the steady liberalization of Yugoslav political life. Although subsequent years have shown a definite softening of this more hardlined stand, the multiethnic condition in Yugoslavia will continue to set outer limits on political change in Yugoslavia.

When looking to the future, it is fair to ask whether continued social mobilization and modernization will soften the ethnocentrism of the Yugoslav peoples, promote a higher sense of Yugoslav community, and therefore, extend the boundaries of permissible political change in Yugoslavia. Although survey research on this question indicates that social mobilization does in fact promote modernism and universalism in the South Slavic context, it is doubtful that this change is significant enough to alter the basic ethnic parameters of Yugoslav politics in the last quarter of this century.[41] While self-management will be furthered and regional decentralization generally respected and maintained, the ethnic groups that comprise Yugoslavia will not be allowed to become independent actors in the Balkan context.

Quantitative and Qualitative Change: A Mobilization or Reconciliation System?

The years of postwar development in Yugoslavia have been marked by far-reaching changes in the characteristics of the population. The people are more literate, more sophisticated, more participant in their values and opinions, and better prepared to take part in the idealized self-managing society. Perhaps to a greater extent than in any other European Communist state, the leaders have instituted political changes intended to take advantage of the new capabilities and interests of the Yugoslav populace. Unlike the arrested change pattern characterizing the developmental processes in the Soviet Union and East European states, the Yugoslav strategy seems to have displayed a genuine willingness to consider and experiment with alternative political forms, many of which were original innovations untried and untested in previous political life. This is not to say that the experimentation was entirely open to whatever alterations intrigued the minds of the innovators. On the contrary, all policies were subject to the cautious approval of the leadership of the LCY, and ultimately, Tito. What did evolve, however, was a process of political change that "signalized the importance of considering, not any particular structure or pattern, but rather the very life processes of the system itself."[42] In contrast to other European Communist leaders, the Yugoslavs follow an enlightened strategy of *system persistence* that showed a genuine willingness to change and adapt to fluctuating circumstances emanating from the diverse and changing Yugoslav environment.

Does this purported change and adaptation in Yugoslavia mean that the system has undergone a qualitative change, or in the words of David Apter, a "system-change"? Has the Yugoslav system moved from the orthodox Leninist-Stalinist mobilization system based upon high levels of coercion and low levels of information to a reconciliation system based upon open information and little coercion? Apter writes: "Let me simply say that it is the relationship between coercion and information which affects changes from one political systems type to another."[43]

In my opinion, Yugoslavia has gone further along the mobilization to reconciliation continuum than any other ruling Communist state. However, it has not made the basic structural change that might allow us to talk of a "system-change"; that is, the party leadership has not relinquished ultimate control of the information and coercion variables, and as a result, the system can not fairly be considered a reconciliation type. What this means is that Yugoslavia has made some far-reaching *quantitative* changes that have exhibited a more open (in terms of information) and less controlled (in terms of coercion) political system. But it has not taken the qualitative leap that would place the control of information and coercion outside of the purview of a single party.

In diagram form, I am contending that Yugoslavia has made significant progress in quantitative terms in moving down the

Figure 2.   Information, Coercion, and Systems Change

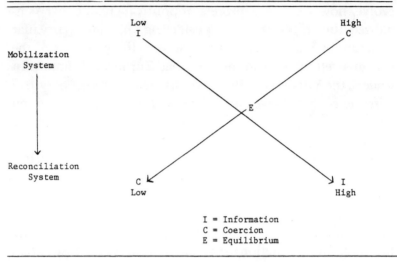

Adapted from Apter, <u>The Politics of Modernization</u>, p. 409.

information and coercion axes (see Figure 2). In the late 1940s Yugoslavia would have been placed at the very top of the diagram; by the 1970s it had moved a good distance toward the bottom. Of course, this trend is not irreversible as was illustrated by the reassertion of LCY control in the early 1970s. In fact, a unilinear trend in any state is probably more an exception than the rule.

Apter notes that to achieve societal goals at minimum cost, a society must find the optimal balance between coercion and information, represented by the point of equilibrium (E) in Figure 2. That Yugoslavia has not yet found this balance is evidenced by occasional uncertainty and policy reversals regarding sociopolitical experimentation and societal decentralization—for example, the response of Tito and the LCY in 1971 to "nationalist deviations" in Croatia and the subsequent removal of a number of high-ranking regional leaders. These reversals are represented as fluctuations on the coercion-information coordinates, and may be interpreted as signs of the country's search for the optimal mixture of the two variables.

Even bearing in mind the so-called retrenchment, or reassertion, of LCY control in 1971, the Yugoslavs appear to have moved far toward the reconciliation system, which Apter describes in the following fashion:

> The role of government in a reconciliation system is not organizational; rather, it works to reconcile diverse interests; it mediates, integrates, and above all, co-ordinates, rather than organizes and mobilizes. In contrast to the mobilization system, which "fights" society, the reconciliation system is often a prisoner of society.[44]

The centrally steered mobilization system, more closely approximating the Soviet system, would resort to whatever forms of coercion and terror deemed necessary by those "from above" to mobilize the society toward ideologically prescribed goals. Information normally existing in the system would be used for purely propaganda purposes to achieve prescribed ends. The low coercion, high information ideal, on the other hand, employs no coercion or terror whatsoever, and hopes that it will move toward regime goals on the basis of total access to the "facts" by unrestricted dissemination of information in an environment of free choice. The underlying philosophy of the latter regime is that change toward societal goals is likely as long as the populace is unrestricted in its access to information.

Needless to say, it is impossible to find an example of this last ideal-type in the contemporary Communist world. However, since the Yugoslav strategy seems to have moved further toward the reconciliation system at a much faster rate than any other Communist state, it may be argued that it has more effectively synchronized the developmental process by educating a literate participant society and implementing structures to facilitate its participatory behaviors. In addition, their willingness to decrease coercion and increase the level of information established an appropriate setting in which the functions of self-government might flourish. In summary, then, although the Yugoslavs have not made the qualitative change to a reconciliation system, they have moved significantly in that direction over the past two decades.

Political Change in Yugoslavia: Evolution of Increasing Civil Strife?

Because the Yugoslavs have tried to synchronize their political development, there appears to be closer correspondence in Yugoslavia between expectations and opportunities regarding power and participation than in other East European states or in the Soviet Union. Although the "administrative period" (1947-52) exhibited little or no increase in value expectations or opportunities, the two subsequent periods of administrative development (1953-64 and 1965 to the present) were marked, despite temporary plateaus, by both growing aspirations and opportunities in all areas of sociopolitical and economic self-management. Therefore, if the theory of relative deprivation and our observations are correct, we might expect less likelihood for revolutionary behavior as a result of power deprivation, and further, a lower propensity for societal instability in Yugoslavia.

However, general impressions of the Yugoslav scene lead many observers to suggest that it is the most unstable of the East European states. Strikes within Yugoslav factories and expressions of discontent within the various regions suggest that feelings of power deprivation do in fact exist. The apparent inconsistency here can be explained by referring once again to the four intervening variables that Gurr maintains are likely to affect the expression and magnitude of civil strife (see Figure 1). For example, with the lowering of coercive potential (Gurr's first variable) that comes with movement toward a reconciliation system, a natural increase in the opportunities and propensity for antisystem behavior is likely to develop. The same situation exists for the remaining three variables affecting the relationship between relative deprivation and social stability. Therefore, while the expectation/opportunity relationship regarding participation suggests lower levels of relative deprivation among the Yugoslav people, the expression of the existing frustration is facilitated and therefore increased.

Conclusion

In conclusion, it seems to me that due to the Soviet Union's reluctance to allow and facilitate genuine participation among the citizens of these other states, the gap is widening between an increasingly sophisticated and conscious citizenry and the political institutions designed for their use. The systems have been successful in the extension of political consciousness to new social groups and the mobilization of these groups into politics, but the political institutions created to allow the people's participation in political life have been neither extensive enough nor meaningful enough to synchronize the developmental process adequately. What has evolved is a controlled or arrested change process marked, at least potentially, by a growing tension (relative deprivation) among the citizenries of these states.

Yugoslavia, on the other hand, following a more enlightened policy, appears to have been more effective in syncronizing the change process. But several points likely to affect the Yugoslav's future need to be remembered. First, movement from a mobilization toward a reconciliation system engenders a more open environment in which frustration and discontent are more easily organized and articulated, thus making the society appear more unstable.

The second point concerns the possibility for a reversal in Yugoslav democratization. Given that Yugoslav society and politics are such that everything is subject to change, the possibility for a decrease in opportunities for participation is always possible. If such a "de-democratization" trend is experienced, the revolutionary potential in Yugoslavia might reach rather dangerous proportions. Davies' "J-curve" hypothesis suggests that "revolutions are most likely to occur when a prolonged period of objective economic and social (or political) development is followed by a short period of reversal.[45] Although such developments are not impossible and the possibility increases when imagining the post-Tito period, the Yugoslavs appear to have reached a point of no return in their process of democratization. To return to the centralization of power and authority of the early years would probably cause many more problems than it would solve.

Notes

1. *Polnoe Sobranie Sochinenii* 33 (Moscow, 1958-65), p. 116.
2. Ibid., p. 253.
3. Ibid., 45, pp. 390-91.
4. Over the years there were some efforts to encourage mass participation and involvement in the political process, but such efforts were largely lacking in authentic, genuine meaning as far as socialist democracy was concerned. In that regard, Gitelman notes: "In line with his vision of the development of Soviet society, Khrushchev abandoned Stalinist mass mobilization and turned to mass participation. But to a large extent, this was inauthentic, pseudo-participation. It was participation without power." See Zvi Gitelman, "Beyond Leninism: Political Development in Eastern Europe," *Newsletter on Comparative Studies of Communism* 5 (1972), p. 24.
5. Such a strategy coincides with the idealized picture of the Communist mobilization system. In that regard, see Chalmers Johnson, ed., *Change in Communist Systems* (Stanford, Calif.: Stanford University Press, 1971), passim.
6. Gitelman, "Beyond Leninism," pp. 24, 32.
7. For the seminal work concerning the synchronization of political change, see Samuel P. Huntington, *Political Order in Changing Societies* (New Haven, Conn.: Yale University Press, 1965). Huntington notes: "The primary problem in politics is the lag in the development of political institutions behind social and economic change." (Ibid., p. 5.) When raising this issue in his study of

participation in the Soviet system, Friedgut speaks of the "destabiliz-
ing elements" that may result from such a lag:

> As the educational and cultural level of the country rises, the
> mobilization of the public and the regime's demands for active
> participation may provide a locus for coalescence of demands upon the
> regime. Increasing sophistication of the citizenry will almost
> inevitably result in a consciousness of lack of autonomy and
> substantive choice in determination of local affairs. The theme of trust
> in adminstrators, trust in parents, trust in youth has already been raised
> in the Soviet press. The common claim of these different groups is that
> they have reached a level of social and political maturity at which they
> are capable of self-sustaining activity without strict control.

Theodore H. Friedgut, "Participation in Soviet Local Government,"
in *Columbia Essays in International Affairs*, Andrew W. Cordier, ed.
(New York: Columbia University Press, 1970), p. 242.

8. Gitelman, "Beyond Leninism," pp. 18-20.

9. For Easton's widely cited definition of system maintenance, see
David Easton, *A Framework for Political Analysis* (Englewood Cliffs,
N.J.: Prentice Hall, 1965), p. 88.

10. Ibid., pp. 77-90.

11. Ibid., p. 88.

12. Gitelman, "Beyond Leninism," pp. 18-19.

13. Other observers are considerably more positive about the extent
of political change and level of popular participation. For the views
of one such observer, see Jerry F. Hough, "Political Participation in
the Soviet Union," *Soviet Studies* 28 (January 1976); and "The
Brezhnev Era: The Man and the System," *Problems of Communism*
25 (March-April 1976).

14. That is, the Soviets have made changes to deal with challenges
emanating from their environment, but it is the nature or content of
such changes that is important. For example, the tightening of
controls on cultural and literary sectors in the 1970s was a change
aimed at system persistence, but by its very nature, was conservative
and acted to broaden still further the disparity between the political
and societal sectors.

15. By speaking of the Soviet and East European states as one
general category, we are of course making undue simplifications and
not allowing for the marked differences that exist among them.
However, for purposes of general discussion and for providing a

frame of reference with which to compare the Yugoslav experience, we feel this is a necessary simplification.

16. Easton, *A Framework for Political Analysis*, pp. 82-85.

17. For a very useful critique of this issue, see Eugene F. Miller, "David Easton's Political Theory," *The Political Science Reviewer* 1 (Fall 1971), pp. 230-32. For a general treatment of Easton's theory, see pp. 184-235.

18. Easton, *A Framework for Political Analysis*, p. 82.

19. For perhaps the most comprehensive and sophisticated development of the idea, see Ted Robert Gurr, *Why Men Rebel* (Princeton, N.J.: Princeton University Press, 1970).

20. Ibid., p. 25.

21. Ibid., pp. 25-26.

22. For purposes of this essay, civil strife is used interchangeably with societal instability.

23. For a discussion of these four factors, see Ted Robert Gurr, "A Causal Model of Civil Strife: A Comparative Analysis Using New Indices," in *Macro-Quantitative Analysis*, Gillespie and Nesvold, eds. (Beverly Hills, Calif.: Sage Publications, 1971), pp. 219-20.

24. For a discussion of the three periods of administrative development in Yugoslavia, see Drago Gorupić, "The Development of the Self-Managing Organization of Enterprises in Yugoslavia," *Yugoslav Survey* 11, no. 3 (1970), pp. 1-16. Gorupić identifies the following periods: 1947-52, centralized administrative management; 1953-64, construction of workers' and social self-management; and, 1965 to the present, further consolidation of the self-managing socialist society.

25. For a discussion and review of the basic principles, functions, and evolution of the workers' councils and workers' self-management in Yugoslavia, see *Workers' Management in Yugoslavia* (Geneva: International Labor Office, 1962); *Participation of Workers in Decisions within Undertakings* (Geneva: International Labor Office, 1967); Ichak Adizes, *Industrial Democracy: Yugoslav Style* (New York: Free Press, 1971); Jiri Kolaja, *Workers' Councils: The Yugoslav Experience* (New York: Praeger, 1965). For Yugoslav sources, see Drago Gorupić, "Tendencije u razvoju radničkog samoupravljanja u Jugoslaviji," *Ekonomist* 20 (Zagreb, 1967), pp. 593-639; Rudi Supek, "Longitudinalno Istrazivanje Struckture Utjecaja u Radničkom Samoupravljanja," (Zagreb: Lipanj, 1971); and K.C. Sethi, "Radničko Samoupravljanje," *Moderna Organizacija* 2 (1971), pp. 145-155.

26. For a consideration of the Yugoslav commune, see Dragoljub

Milivajević, *The Yugoslav Commune* (Belgrade: Medunarodna Politika, 1965), Studies no. 8; Jovan Djordjević and Najdan Pasić, "The Communal System of Self-Government in Yugoslavia," *International Social Science Journal* 13, no. 3 (1961), pp. 390-405; and Gerry Hunnius, "The Yugoslav System of Decentralization and Self-Management," in *The Case for Participatory Democracy*, Benello and Roussopoulos, eds. (New York: Viking, 1971), pp. 140-77.

27. The 1974 constitution and 1976 Law on Associated Labor, often referred to as Yugoslavia's mini-constitution, outline the rights and obligations of self-management in almost excessive detail.

28. For an interesting discussion of the nature of worker self-management and the certain controversies over decison-making questions, see Ivan Paj, "The Organization of Self-Management in Enterprises," *Yugoslav Survey* 12, no. 1 (February 1971), pp. 31-50.

29. For a consideration of the problems of inadequate expertise and information, poor communication, and insecurity among the workers, and a number of other problems related to worker participation, see Drago Gorupić, "Aktuelni Problemi Radničkog Samoupravljanja," *Ekonomski Pregled* 22, no. 1 (1971), pp. 93-100.

30. Hunnius, "The Yugoslav System," p. 164.

31. For critical discussion of this and other important questions concerning the Yugoslav experience, see G. David Garson, *On Democratic Administration and Socialist Self-Management: A Comparative Survey Emphasizing the Yugoslav Experience* (Beverly Hills, Calif.: Sage Publications, 1974); Sharon Zukin, *Beyond Marx and Tito: Theory and Practice in Yugoslav Socialism* (New York: Cambridge University Press, 1975); and Branko Horvat et al., *Self-Governing Socialism* (White Plains, N.Y.: International Arts and Sciences Press, 1975).

32. Krste Crvenkovski, "Divorcing the Party from Power," *Socialist Thought and Practice* 25 (1967), pp. 40-49.

33. See Paul Lendvai's excellent discussion, "The Party in Search of a Role," *Eagles in Cobwebs* (Garden City, N.Y.: Anchor Books, 1969), pp. 146-70.

34. Dennison I. Rusinow, "Yugoslavia's Return to Leninism," *Fieldstaff Reports*, Southeast Europe Series, vol. 21, no. 1, 1974.

35. Remark of LCY Secretary Stane Dolanc, *Ideological and Political Offensive of the League of Communists of Yugoslavia* (Belgrade, 1972), p. 46.

36. Bogdan Denis Denitch, *The Legitimation of a Revolution: The Yugoslav Case* (New Haven, Conn.: Yale University Press, 1976), passim.

37. Josip Obradovic and Gary Bertsch, "Moć i Odgovornost U Samoupravnom Socijalizmu," *Nase Teme* 18 (November 1974), pp. 1895-1917.

38. Susan Lampland Woodward, "Socialization for Self-Management in Yugoslav Schools," *Comparative Communism: The Soviet, Chinese, and Yugoslav Models,* Gary K. Bertsch and Thomas W. Ganschow, eds. (San Francisco: W.H. Freeman, 1976).

39. For a comprehensive treatment of Yugoslav nationalities policy, see Paul Shoup, *Communism and the Yugoslav National Question* (New York: Columbia University Press, 1968).

40. Gary K. Bertsch, "The Revival of Nationalisms," *Problems of Communism* 22, no. 7 (November - December 1973), pp. 1-16.

41. Gary K. Bertsch, *Values and Community in Multi-National Yugoslavia* (New York: Columbia University Press, 1976).

42. Gitelman, "Beyond Leninism," p. 88.

43. David Apter, *The Politics of Modernization* (Chicago: University of Chicago Press, 1965), p. vi.

44. Ibid., pp. 398-99.

45. James C. Davies, "Toward a Theory of Revolution," *American Sociological Review* 27 (February 1962), p. 6.

7

Thirty Years of Crisis Management in Poland

Jan T. Gross

French historian Alain Besançon begins his *Short Treatise of Sovietology for Military, Civilized and Religious Authorities* by stating that in the study of Communist society one undertakes a task unlike any other: one attempts to comprehend and explain a phenomenon that is by all criteria of logic and rationality incomprehensible and absurd.[1] I need not dwell on the absurd quality of a myriad of official government policies in the Communist countries for they are well known. Nevertheless I want to allude at the outset of my essay to this peculiar quality of the Soviet society that, for sixty years now, has challenged the analytic powers of some of the best scholarly minds in the free world. My subject here is conflict management in Poland—a Soviet-dominated society—and as such calls for an assessment of the adaptability and therefore of the future of the Polish regime. Of course, any assessment of the future of such regimes is even more risky than an attempt to understand their past accomplishments. For if one ventures beyond the mere statement that those regimes have been where they are for thirty or sixty years as the case may be, and that they are going to stay there for the foreseeable future, one joins the ranks of those who, on many occasions in the past, predicted their downfall or radical transformation and were proved wrong. And yet to think of those regimes as permanent fixtures and not bother with controversial predictions defies intellec-

tual curiosity. Should one, however, express loudly the belief
that Soviet regimes are subject to internal decay and are on the
way to "devolution," one risks ridicule on the part of
knowledgeable foreign policy experts, most of whom, including very eminent ones, perceive Soviet societies and regimes as
robust and expanding.

And yet, even though the fate of similar predictions in the
past should make me cautious, and the opposite views
predominant in powerful political circles today perhaps
should make me wary, I am convinced that the future of the
Communist regimes is rather gloomy. Of course, I have no
foolproof argument to support my beliefs, but then "it is
absurd to expect an end to absurdity. Otherwise absurdity
would be consequential and finite and would no longer be
absurdity. Absurdity has no end; it will just break off at one of
its absurd links when no one expects it to. And it won't break
off because the absurdity has come to an end but because the
meaningful has a beginning, and that beginning excludes and
annuls the absurd."[2]

Since I am going to talk about an end of absurdity and the
beginning of the meaningful, I find great comfort in these
words of Boris Pasternak, which I understand as a dispensa-
tion: one could never hope to prove that the end of the Soviet
type of society is about to come; one can only look for signs.

The problem of crisis management cannot be carved out as a
distinct subject in the study of the Polish People's Republic. It
is simply that her entire history, from 1944 to the present, is one
of long, procrastinating crisis. The proof of this may be
obtained from official Polish government publications—in all
appearance the source least likely to carry such information.
But it is there that we first read about the critical early years of
implementing the socialist revolution and the armed struggle
with the "fascist and reactionary" underground. Then in the
same media there followed in quick succession a condemnation
of Gomułka's rightist-nationalist deviation. In 1955-56 readers
of the party-controlled press were fed criticism of Stalinism

only to be warned a few years later about the dangers of revisionism, which constituted yet another critical threat to the regime the authorities effectively headed off. Upon Gierek's ascent to power, the early sixties were castigated for their zero growth and exceptionally bad management of the economy, as the late sixties acquired notoriety for the leadership's inability to remain in touch with the masses—a major crisis in itself. And the time will soon come, probably on the occasion of the investiture of the next first secretary, to learn about unsolved critical problems during Gierek's tenure. Thus, in a rather paradoxical twist of fate, party-controlled propaganda gives justice, though always with a few years' delay, to the quality of party rule in Poland.

These observations should not be taken lightly for they suggest, implicitly, a methodological directive for any social scientist interested in studying crisis management in Poland: in order to find out about his subject, he would be ill-advised to focus exclusively on such characteristic moments as October 1956, March 1968, or December 1970. This is not to deny that historical moments designated by those dates carry some special meaning. Those were, indeed, moments of heightened intensity and visibility of social conflicts in Poland. But at the same time, upon closer scrutiny, one discovers that they were something else as well—namely, brief periods of communication, as it were, between the authorities and the society. There was, then, a momentary suspension of the routine mode of operation of the system: the scope of political participation was significantly broadened and the stage was set for some open expression of discontent and anger; the collective bond within the polity was partially restored. Through the communal experience of "discussion," "consultation," or "congregation," the somewhat depleted legitimacy of the existing order was recreated and the mandate designed to support the existing authority pattern through the next stretch of relative stability and social peace was strengthened.

It seems, at first glance, rather strange that moments of

heightened tension and increased discontent, agitation and protest *against* the regime, could be functional *for* the regime. But the regime seems to emerge strengthened from those confrontations without having fundamentally reformed itself: it neither relinquishes its exclusive grip on power nor becomes capable of aggregating, articulating, representing, or acting on the interests and aspirations of the vast majority of the population. In addition to replenishing its legitimacy by virtue of its renewed confrontation with the populace, the regime also accomplishes necessary changes that otherwise could not be implemented, such as rotation of the top echelon, in particular, the position of the first secretary. In people's democracies, with a few minor exceptions, death in office, a palace revolution, or a major breakdown is still needed for the overhaul of the top political elite. Making such overhaul possible is yet another contribution of periodic breakdowns to the maintenance of the regime.

In sum, I propose to conceptualize the history of the Communist regime in Poland in terms exactly opposite to those ordinarily applied to this task. Stretches of time typically looked upon as periods of relative normalization and social peace I propose to present as characterized by unresolved underlying conflicts and building tensions. Periods of breakdown, I would like to suggest, should be studied, on the other hand, for their contribution to conflict resolution and tension release.

I perceive three types of strategies used by the Communist authorities in Poland to cope with what they probably consider to be unusually difficult and thorny political, social, and economic problems. One strategy is to repress directly, sometimes annihilate physically, those groups or individuals perceived as threatening to the regime. This policy was applied systematically during the period of the Communist takeover of the country. Arrests, deportations into Russia, and executions of Polish patriots belonging to the so-called London underground were initially carried out by the NKVD (Soviet secret police) with full cooperation of the Polish Communists and later continued by the Polish Security Forces under NKVD's supervision. The cornerstone of People's Poland is the mass grave of 200,000 Poles from Warsaw, whom the Soviets watched being slaughtered during the 1944 uprising without offering any help. In this way the Germans liquidated the brain and muscle of the patriotic conspiratorial network that would have later, without doubt, opposed the sovietization of the country. Then well into the fifties, under a thin veil of Stalinist legality, the survivors of the patriotic antifascist underground were being tracked down, imprisoned, and executed. Simultaneously the so-called class enemies—the prewar bourgeoisie, the landowning gentry, and the intelligentsia—were very often deprived of material means of subsistence, relegated to petty jobs, their children denied access to higher education. All of them were condemned to a rather precarious existence where one imprudent conversation often meant the difference between imprisonment and freedom. The worst crimes and abuses ended after Stalin's death, but the restoration of physical terror as a method of quenching popular protest has taken place intermittently since: suffice it to mention the mass killings of workers in December 1970 or the beatings and tortures after the June 1976 food riots.

I would like to call the second strategy of coping with particularly difficult or explosive situations symbolic manipulation. To this category belongs, for example, the spurious plurality of organizations maintained by the Communist authorities in an effort to confuse the population of the country and outside observers about the true monolithic nature of the Polish political regime. Thus Bolesław Piasecki, Poland's most eminent prewar fascist, bought his life in exchange for an offer to create, under the government's sponsorship, a lay Catholic and, at the same time, "progressive" organization, PAX, that could counterbalance the influence of the Church in Poland and prevent effective mobilization of Catholics against the regime. Similarly, when forced by international agreements to tolerate an independent peasant party in Poland for a few years after the end of the war, the Communists also sponsored a number of other "progressive" peasant, socialist, and democratic parties in order to confuse the electorate as well as public opinion abroad.

Another distinct application of the strategy of symbolic manipulation consists in denying that social conflicts exist by refusing to name them. This is one of the fundamental applications of the regime's exclusive control over the mass media. It is a well-established tenet in political sociology that unless feelings of social deprivation are translated and articulated by political leaders into clearly formulated programs of political revindication, there is little likelihood that the subjugated group can resort to collective remedial action. People as individuals in modern society are very confused as to what may be the source of their grief and discomfort. They need at least the opportunity to discuss their individual problems before they can translate them into statements of collective deprivations and then act on them. Naturally the regime sees no reason to make this possible.

Symbolic manipulation is also involved when, through a concerted propaganda effort, various scapegoats are promoted in order to release accumulated social tension and direct society's attention away from substantive problems that the government could not attend to without loosening its exclusive grip on power. Again examples are numerous, the most spectacular one perhaps being the trick of labeling Stalinism as a period of "mistakes and distortions," whereby a serious discussion of compatibility between freedom and the one-party system was avoided; or stirring up anti-Semitism in 1968 in hopes that the population, by observing Moczar and his sycophants climb to power, would in some vicarious way share in this upward mobility and forget about the stagnation of the sixties.

Neither repression nor deception but unification is the third strategy for coping with accumulated social conflicts in a

Communist society. During the recent party conference, Gierek repeated a line with which over the last thirty-five years the Polish population has grown too familiar: "To continue our forward march, to take on obstacles, we must unify our thoughts and efforts; the hearts of all Poles must beat in one rhythm." One may ask what lies behind this line of argument that makes it so attractive to the Communist rulers of Poland as to be endlessly repeated in their speeches? Why do they see in unification a miraculous panacea for crisis management in Poland?

Naturally any proposed solution must derive from the proponent's understanding of the nature of the problem to be resolved. What is the nature of the problem, then, if in order to deal with it effectively all Poles must get together?

I believe these demagogic appeals for national unity derive from the premise that a clear-cut hierarchy of priorities exists in the politics of a given community. It stipulates implicitly that in this hierarchy at least the top priority is agreed upon by the overwhelming majority of the population. Faced with this priority, all divisions within society must fade; all groups in society must put aside any consideration of their particularistic interests lest they jeopardize the good of all, lest they betray the common interest. What possibly could constitute such a priority so indisputably shared by so many? Only one thing in the life of a community could have such an overwhelming quality—its very existence, meaning for a modern nation-state its sovereignty and independence.

But if there is a threat to Polish sovereignty today, then where does it come from? In the last sixty years only Nazi Germany and the Soviet Union posed such a threat to Poland. Nazi Germany was defeated long ago, and as for the Soviet threat, I doubt that it is on the minds of the Communist rulers of Poland when they make appeals for national unity.

Gierek's appeals for national unity, as those of his predecessors, do not represent a sincere effort to cope with the growth pains being suffered by People's Poland. These appeals do not result from an analysis of the social conflicts and tensions accompanying modernization and change in Polish society, nor do they follow from any real sense of endangered national sovereignty. They are mere propaganda gimmicks that are rather well chosen in view of the turbulent history of Polish statehood in the last two centuries. Through these appeals Communist rulers are tapping the nationalistic feelings of the Poles and, only too often, their xenophobia.

It is not accidental, I might add, that propaganda themes explored by the Communist party to mobilize mass support for its policies resemble the watchwords of radical nationalists. This is so because followers of the ideology of the National Democratic party and the defenders of the monoparty regime ruling Poland today—with their numerous differences—share a distaste for all organized manifestations of social plurality. A solidaristic vision of a nation and totalitarian vision of a society have in common their denial of legitimacy to social plurality and differentiation. No wonder that in its political conception national democracy views with mistrust the institutional framework of parliamentary democracy and opts for one-party solutions. Similarly, monoparty regimes sooner (like Germany or Italy) or later (like the USSR or Poland) make appeals to the feelings of aggressive nationalism either by cherishing the imperial past and power of a Moscow or a Rome, or, in the satellite countries, by feeding obscurantism and xenophobia. Sometimes this is done openly—for instance when popular anti-Semitism was unleashed under the guise of anti- Zionism—and at other times half openly—as when anti-German or even anti-Russian feelings of the population were manipulated. Thus, in a curious convergence, those two politico-ideological movements eventually betray their original premises: a revolutionary tool for implementing a distinct class interest becomes a spokesman of national solidarity, and the spokesman for a whole nation becomes a proponent of one-party rule.

Yet, strangely, none of it seems to work. In spite of exclusive control over the economy, police, state bureaucracy, legislature, mass media, educational system, and everything else having any impact on the organization of collective life, the regime in Poland seems uniquely incapable of steering clear of trouble. Why is there a protracted social crisis in Poland if, seemingly, all instruments for crisis resolution are available and concentrated in the hands of the government?

In my view the regime in Poland possesses neither adequate information nor adequate manpower to formulate and enforce policies that would promote conflict resolution in the Polish society. To put it differently, it does not blunder simply because its policies are guided by some ideological goals different from public preferences; its difficulties are not merely a calculated and accepted cost of the attempt to change people's preferences, to teach them new attitudes, and to socialize them into new patterns of behavior. The protracted crisis is not then a more or less predicted cost of a planned reform. To the contrary the crisis results, as I will try to show, from the lack of information as to what the social preferences are and the system's inability to generate such information. These are major obstacles against overcoming the crisis. They induce a fundamentally conservative outlook in the decision makers who, fearing that they cannot foresee the consequences of their policy decisions, tend to avoid launching any reform or innovations. They fail to act because, in the first place, unanticipated consequences of a reform may easily spell greater trouble for the system than those due to the difficulties the reform was supposed to overcome. Second, since there is little hope of finding effective solutions to problems, the tendency is to stick to the routine until some major breakdown occurs. As it is less obvious who bears responsibility for "old ways," it is safer for men in the organization not to become identified as innovators, i.e., sitting ducks whose responsibility for new policies may be easily ascertained.

The lack of adequate manpower, another cause of the protracted crisis, is the consequence of decades of negative selection on all levels of the party structure that effectively weeded out most individuals with initiative, creativity, independent judgment, and moral integrity who, out of naiveté, enthusiasm, or temperament, decided to join the party in order to lead politically active lives. Instead obedience and narrow-mindedness are the qualities insuring prompt promotion in the ranks of party organization. Stanisław Ossowski used the expression "unbending conformist" when speaking about the dominant character trait of one such careerist who was also a university professor. As Merle Fainsod has put it: "The prototype of the ideal Bolshevik whom the party leadership seeks to fashion and create is essentially that of a dedicated subordinate. . . . The operational philosophy of Communism is designed to breed willing robots whose 'freedom' is exercised in ingenious and energetic efforts to discharge the tasks which the party leadership assigns to them."[3] Altogether the party forum provides an ideal environment for mediocrities—because mediocrity shines there as a star of the first order.

This phenomenon of negative selection is not merely a flaw of the regime convenient for its critics and satirists whom it provides with anecdotal evidence of the rulers' boorishness and ineptitude. For social scientists it represents a formidable challenge because it flies in the face of what most political theorists seem to have agreed upon: from Aristotle until today they have expressed the conviction that a political system without procedures for leadership recruitment, unable to tap and promote merit and aptitude, is fundamentally unstable and doomed to internal decay and overthrow by a counterelite.

Here, then, is a major theme to explore in sociological analysis: How, with an institutionalized mechanism for recruiting mediocrity (at best) into the leadership, did the system survive so long? Are political scientists and foreign policymakers in the West correct in their appraisal of the Soviet bloc as robust, expanding, and disciplined with a future that will overshadow our own? Or are the dissidents correct when they speak of unresolved and unresolvable problems in Soviet bloc societies; of structural inadequacies that are bound to breed popular discontent endlessly; of waste, fear, and discomfort that alienate ever more people from the regime? Is Amalryk correct in his prediction that this regime must disintegrate soon, perhaps in the next decade, or is Henry Kissinger correct with his sobering view that the West must negotiate a deal with the Soviet Union while it still can, before it succumbs to its own anarchy and the Soviet Union's bustling vitality? It does not even help to say that all state bureaucracies breed a mentality of obedience and conservatism. or that they tend to screen and promote uncritical followers fit to obey, but never to lead or initiate. Even if this were true, the socialist countries of today would still be uniquely affected because of the totalitarian claims of their regimes. There the state or the party organization pervades the entire social body and thus deprives society of independent economic, legislative, judiciary, or intellectual establishments that, in a pluralist system, provide a steady flow of talent into the political elite.

That totalitarian claims of the regime are no longer strictly enforced matters little from the point of view of conflict management. First of all there are no institutional guarantees that a return to strict enforcement could not be made at any moment. Such a return may be impractical or difficult for the authorities, but it would be neither a constitutional nor a legal problem—merely a praxeological one. Second, I would argue that as long as social conflict cannot be recognized, i.e., legitimately expressed and named as such, conditions for its management are lacking: it can be, in conditions of illegitimacy, either repressed or mismanaged. Third, a totalitarian state even though ideally capable of total control and total mobilization is also, so to speak, totally vulnerable. Even a mere indication of a desire for privacy, a mere inaction, constitutes, in view of the total claim on people's lives, a challenge to the legitimacy of such a state, and if tolerated, must lead to the erosion of this legitimacy. This, to be sure, does

not promote the ability for conflict management. Instead, it
dramatically limits response options available to the government. In a totalist state there is little difference between a group
of people signing a protest against a government-proposed
amendment to the constitution and an angry crowd shouting
against an increase in meat prices. In both instances the
legitimacy of the regime is at stake, and both parties to the
conflict know it. Thus, a tremendous overload results and there
is little ability to discriminate between one conflict and another
as each strike, each student rally, each "price regulation"
brings, what we would call in America, a "constitutional
crisis." If people cannot go on strike without risking being
killed or tortured, if suspension of a play's production cannot
be protested without hundreds of students risking expulsion
from the university, and if a price increase cannot be
implemented without several promotions and demotions in
the cabinet, then, clearly, the system is ill-suited to manage
social conflict.

The Marxist vision of collective life is predicated upon two
corollary presuppositions: (1) that the only basis for social
differentiation leading towards the emergence of distinct group
identity is the people's position vis-à-vis the means of
production, and (2) that all competition for political power is
illegitimate because it derives solely from different class
interests and, therefore, from exploitation. Thus the denial of
social plurality, the totalitarian legitimacy, comes naturally:
allegedly, with the private ownership of the means of
production abolished, there is no more exploitation in society
and, ipso facto, no more class conflict. The social basis for
competing claims over political power in society is, by
definition, eradicated.

Whether many people believe in this ideological construct
today is of secondary importance. Enough believed in it for the
revolution, or a takeover, to be carried out in its time. And even
though the initial idealism of many faded, one thing
remained—the organizational weapon, the monopoly over

political power in society exercised by the Communist party.

Thus politically, for a variety of reasons, the Communist revolution succeeded—in a partial validation of Marxist analysis, the Communist party took power and holds exclusive control over it. Sociologically, however, Marxist analysis failed: it did not come true that as a consequence of socializing the means of production, "administration over things" slowly replaced "government over men." Society did not cease in October 1917 in Russia or in July 1944 in Poland, and it becomes increasingly more obvious to everyone, including the power holders, that social processes continue spontaneous and uncontrollable and that they generate a plurality of social forces that have to be reckoned with and cannot be liquidated by administrative means.

Here is the contradiction, then, that in my view makes conflict management in the Soviet bloc societies impossible: an organization designed and fit to combat class enemies in a divided society, or to provide for the needs of members of a classless, solidary society, is faced with a reality that was never supposed to occur—competing claims of a plurality of social groups in a society where the private ownership of the means of production was abolished. If the regime wishes to maintain its control over power and decision making, it must literally construe a representation of reality in which it can justifiably function. It must either deny that any such competing claims exist in order to pretend that it indeed rules over a solidary society, or label all such claims as illegitimate, unjustified, reactionary, unpatriotic—in a word, as anachronisms reminiscent of the old class conflict. This is indeed what is happening: social conflict in the socialist society is either denied or decried by the power holders as conspiratorial. As a result, a variety of social processes and social forces can no longer be accommodated by the existing institutional setup. Increasingly larger chunks of people's actions, desires, and thoughts are expressed outside the framework of the official institutions. And this is an ill omen for the regime for, as Karl Deutsch correctly noted, although "governments can modify communities in rare and favorable situations, on the whole it is the communities which make governments."[4]

Thus, to repeat the point I made earlier: the most formidable obstacle preventing leaders of today's Poland from proposing viable solutions to its problems is that they lack information about virtually every aspect of life in the country. Having imposed one-party rule and centralized economy, having abolished independent labor unions and voluntary associations, having forced outward conformity upon society with a network of police informers, the regime has pushed authentic, spontaneous collective life outside of the framework of official institutions. Consequently, the regime in Poland, like all other governments of the so-called people's democracies, finds itself in a serious predicament. For those regimes are, figuratively speaking, cut off from their own societies. Insulated by powerful bureaucracies that are interested primarily in self-perpetuation, they know less and less about the true nature of interests, aspirations, fears, and preferences of the existing and newly forming social forces in the complex modern societies over which they rule. By imposing an ostensible uniformity and obedience, they do not prevent social initiatives from developing and various group interests from being pursued. Rather, by denying legitimacy to this authentic social plurality, they induce interest groups to manipulate the system by feeding it with slanted information in order to extract from it favorable rulings and force them to circumvent the existing institutions, to articulate outside of the officially sanctioned establishment. Consequently, with the passage of time, the authorities have a completely distorted representation of reality, and they cannot do anything about it because accurate information regarding important resources in such a society is simply not available.

One could, perhaps, argue that it matters little because, after all, despotic governments are by definition not supposed to be troubled by their inability to read and therefore satisfy the preferences of their subjects. But the truth of the matter is that a government needs information about public preferences and resources not only in order to cater to public tastes, but also in order to manipulate the public. And this is the reason why the social vacuum in which an authoritarian government finds itself is so incapacitating—such a government cannot even plan to reform itself because it is incapable of predicting the consequences of any reform. It is paralyzed by having lost the capacity to predict the consequences of its actions; it can only respond to breakdowns because it has lost the ability to anticipate.

Where in this broad picture of conflict management in Poland does the opposition fit? Allow me to sketch a brief historical outline of the last twenty years in the Soviet bloc countries as this should permit us to grasp the meaning of the changing role of the regime's political opponents.

The character and timing of liberalization that followed Stalin's death was different in different countries of the Soviet bloc. In the Soviet Union it culminated with Khrushchev's secret speech during the Twentieth Party Congress; in Budapest it led to a proclamation of neutrality and a bloodbath when the Red Army invaded the country; in Prague it took twelve years for de-Stalinization to run its course, and a Soviet military invasion was required in August 1968 to put an end to socialism with a human face; in Warsaw the climax came in October 1956 with the elevation to power of Władysław Gomułka.

Clearly, de-Stalinization spelled trouble for the party apparatus in the Soviet bloc countries and was handled only with the utmost difficulty. But (and I think this is true generally, not just in the case of Poland) the ruling Communist parties submitted themselves of their own volition to the process of de-Stalinization. In each country it came about as a result of pressure from the party apparatus itself, eager to throw off the yoke of the security police, which had grown from the position of watchdog over society to a dominating force threatening the party bureaucracy itself. However, since the party and the police were woven together intimately, this was not a matter of simple surgery. The total organism was infected, and no single part of the social body could be removed to cure the evil. Thus, in the process of de-Stalinization, society was unavoidably awakened, and various groups and individuals proceeded to speak with their own voices demanding reinstatement of freedom and liberalization for all. From the point of view of the Communist party, this was not a desired outcome. It was, rather, an unanticipated consequence, a necessary evil, to be stopped as soon as possible. When it proved impossible to control this process of spontaneous democratization, Soviet tanks rolled into the streets. In Warsaw, as it turned out, this was not necessary—Gomułka was able to handle the job by himself.

Of course the regime changed in Poland after Stalin's death; in particular the use of physical terror was abandoned. But in one respect it remained the same: the ruling party never intended to give up its hegemony over society. In the period of transition to the new phase—absolutism without torture— freedom of speech and democratization crept in. But they were unwanted and slowly blotted out. In October the party finally regained full control over the process, and it proceeded to steer, under Gomułka's leadership, in the direction of new stabilization, later called "our small stabilization." In short, in the years 1954-56 the system changed on the initiative primarily of the power elite, and not so much under the pressure of the opposition.

In 1968, during the so-called March events, there was not only provocation by anti-Semitic elements in the party and the police, but also opposition from the intelligentsia and the students.[5] In December 1970 elements of provocation could still be seen, but above all there was a wave of workers' strikes, and that meant a workers' opposition powerful enough to force a change in the government and a change in policy—the price increase was rolled back after months of negotiations and strikes. In 1975-76 the intelligentsia and the workers stood up against the government in rapid sequence. First the intelligentsia organized protests against proposed changes in the constitution, and then workers marched into the streets in protest against another attempt to raise prices, which, consequently, did not take place. After June 1976 the intelligentsia and the workers joined in a common front symbolized by the setting up of the Workers' Defense Committee.

There has been a clearly discernible change in the scenario of these crises. They recur at ever shorter intervals, and as time goes by, the system's changes occur more in response to the actions of the opposition, and less as the result of manipulation by the power elite. The power elite loses control over the process of change. Change is imposed upon it by social forces slowly emancipating themselves from tutelage. One may describe this process from a different perspective by pointing out that the regime is becoming alienated from ever more groups in Polish society. After 1968 it could no longer count on the "progressive intelligentsia"; after 1970 it began to fear the workers; and since 1976 it has been opposed by a coalition of workers, intelligentsia, and the Catholic episcopate. Throughout the last twenty years, from 1956 to 1977, the regime has been slowly sinking into a social vacuum as the opposition emerges from isolation, slowly gaining consciousness of itself as a united, though pluralistic and internally diversified, political movement.

Today the democratic movement in Poland—with its numerous periodicals, with its alternative university, its independent student organization, its bureau of intervention where citizens lodge complaints against injustices suffered at the hands of the authorities—constitutes perhaps the most important political development in the Soviet bloc countries since 1945.[6] For the first time on such a scale, the *pays réel* behind the iron curtain takes recognizable shape and confronts the *pays légal*. In an interview with *Les Temps Modernes*, Jacek Kuroń recently gave the following explanation of the meaning and role of the opposition in Poland: "In a totalitarian or an occupied country two forms of opposition were traditionally recognized—conspiracy aiming at the overthrow of the imposed regime and efforts to induce the authorities to do some 'beneficial' things. Since the activities of the Workers' Defense Committee are not conspiratorial, they are interpreted as a form of pressure on the authorities. . . . But we indulge in a completely new form of activity. We are oriented in our actions towards society and not towards the authorities. Through our doings it is the society which organizes itself independently of the state power."[7] This is the novelty then—the re-creation of civic society in the midst of a totalitarian system. I believe that what we are observing in Poland, though a novelty in a Soviet bloc country, is merely another episode of the unfolding democratic revolution taking place all over the world, wherever societies are constricted by authoritarian governments. Spain, Portugal, Greece, and India are the most striking examples of polities where the emancipation of society from its government has taken place. And there is a common theme in all these revolutions transcending the difference in political realities of each country—the restoration of social pluralism and legitimacy of political democracy.

Today in Poland the democratic movement draws into its ranks the best people from all walks of life. It speaks about people's real problems since it can sustain itself only as long as it formulates and provides for authentic needs of the social milieus it comes in contact with. On both accounts—as far as the quality of its manpower and the quality of its information about social problems is concerned—the opposition movement today is the opposite of the regime. It attracts the elite of the future; it keeps informed about the social ills to be mended and about social preferences as to how this should be accomplished.

In conclusion, there is no hope for effective conflict management in Poland unless the opposition becomes, to some degree, institutionalized. Unless this is accomplished the ruling elite will lose what remains of its ability to manipulate the public. Some will certainly notice that this would mean an effective limitation on the monopoly of power that the regime holds at present and to which it would therefore never consent. But in fact the regime is no longer free to do as it pleases, for it is the formula of the opposition to act and induce other people to act as free men in a free country. "But liberty," said Edmund Burke in his *Reflections on the Revolution in France,* "when men act in bodies, is power."[8]

Notes

1. Alain Besançon, *Court traité de soviétologie: à l'usage des autorités civiles, militaires et religieuses* (Paris: Hachette, 1976), p. 15.

2. "The Unpublished Letters of Boris Pasternak," *New York Times Magazine,* January 1, 1978, p. 12.

3. Merle Fainsod, *How Russia Is Ruled* (Cambridge, Mass.: Harvard University Press, 1963),pp. 213, 215.

4. Karl Deutsch, *Nationalism and Social Communication* (Cambridge, Mass.: MIT Press, 1966), p. 78.

5. For a full documentation concerning the "March" events, see *Wydarzenia Marcowe 1968* (Instytut Literacki, Paryż, 1969); *Polskie Przedwiośnie. Dokumentów Marcowych t.II.* (Instytut Literacki, Paryż, 1969); Marek Tarniewski, *Krótkie Spięcie* (Instytut Literacki Paryż, 1977).

6. Full coverage and commentary of political developments in Poland is provided by the Paris monthly *Kultura* and the London-based quarterly *Aneks.* In addition a collection of documents of the Polish democratic movement was published by *Kultura: Ruch Oporu* (Instytut Literacki, Paryż, 1977). There is an English language collection of documents, *Dissent in Poland, 1976-77,* Association of Polish Students and Graduates in Exile, 42 Emperors Gate, London SW7, 1977; and a recent publication in French, *La Pologne: une société en dissidence,* Z. Erard and G. M. Zygier, eds. (Paris: François Maspero, 1978).

7. Jacek Kuroń, *Les Temps Modernes,* no. 1 (1977), reprinted in Z. Erard and G.M. Zygier, *La Pologne,* p. 17.

8. Edmund Burke, *Reflections on the Revolution in France* (Garden City, N.J.: Doubleday and Co., Dolphin Books, 1961), p. 20.

8
Ethnicity and Change in the Soviet Union

Teresa Rakowska-Harmstone

The international and popular Western image of the Soviet Union rarely recognizes the multiethnic and formally federal character of the Soviet state. The usual perception is that the Soviet Union is synonymous with "Russia." This is so, first, because in the Soviet Union the Russians are the dominant nation, quantitatively and qualitatively, their historical hegemony having survived intact the 1917 revolution and the transition from imperial Russia to the Soviet "international workers' " state; second, because the highly centralized nature of the Soviet political system, run by the unitary Communist party, renders the federal constitutional state structure largely irrelevant for the purposes of international realpolitik. Only rarely is one reminded of the federal nature of the USSR, as in the case of Soviet demands to grant full United Nations' status to all of its constituent national republics, or an attempt to have one or another republic acting as a sovereign state in the international arena for selective (and transient) foreign policy purposes,[1] which in the sixties and seventies, for example, resulted in a higher profile for the Soviet Muslim republics. But, as the flow of exchanges and data between the Soviet

Reprinted from "Ethnic Conflict in the World Today" in vol. 43 (September 1977) of *The Annals* of The American Academy of Political and Social Sciences.

Union and the West has increased in the post-Stalin era, the phenomenon of ethnicity (the old-fashioned term used in the Soviet Union is "the national problem") and the presence of ethnic conflict there have become increasingly visible.

The ethnic conflict in the Soviet Union does not take the form of an open conflict of a kind present in many other multiethnic societies throughout the world. The very nature of the Soviet political system precludes that. Marxist-Leninist ideology, which is the source of legitimacy for the monopoly of power the CPSU exercises in the country, denies the existence of conflicts other than those based in class exploitation, and postulates, ex cathedra, that with the achievement of socialism the class and ethnic conflicts in the USSR have both disappeared. The theory is that the unity of the Soviet nations and nationalities stems from the class-based "proletarian internationalism" (all Soviet citizens, of whatever nationality, are the "working people") and that the "national problem" in the Soviet Union has been solved precisely because of the duality of the Soviet political system. The national character of each ethnic group is safeguarded in the constitutional national form, but their overriding class-based unity, the socialist content, is expressed by the leading role of the CPSU—the "toilers" vanguard and the leading force in society. Consequently, any open ethnic self-assertion which transgresses the limits of the "national form–socialist content" formula is suppressed. But the dichotomy also opens up the avenues for "legitimate" self-assertion.

The nature and appearance of ethnic conflict in the Soviet Union are therefore different than in other more open societies. On the one hand, the systemic constraints prevent expression of open separatism as well as open ethnic warfare. For this reason there is no agreement among experts whether the highly visible phenomenon of ethnic self-assertion by major Soviet ethnic groups can be defined as nationalism. On the other hand, the legal framework of the system and its ideological premises not only allow the pursuit of ethnic autonomy, but also preempt the option of a return to an imperial state based on Russian nationalism, even though de facto the new Soviet value system and patterns of behavior are permeated—for historical reasons—by the Russian political culture content.

In the Soviet Union, therefore, the forces of ethnicity find their expression within the system, and the ethnic conflict is regulated by the rules imposed by it. The Russians and the Ukrainians or the Uzbeks, for example, do not fight in the streets; on the contrary, professions of "unbreakable unity" and "fraternal ties" fill the Soviet media, resound in conferences and assemblies, provide the message in the arts, and form the keynote of official pronouncements. Yet, at the same time the whole fabric of Soviet society is permeated, subtly but unmistakably, by ethnic antagonisms and competition between the dominant Russians and all others in political, economic, social, and cultural life.

All available evidence indicates that the rate of growth of the national self-assertion of major Soviet ethnic groups exceeds their rate of assimilation into a common Soviet value system. The problem, while not officially acknowledged, is recognized by the Soviet leadership. In the words of one of the key Politburo leaders, ethnic antagonisms constitute one of the three main obstacles on the "road to building communism."[2] In the opinion of this writer, the ethnic conflict is now the major force for change in the Soviet Union. It presents no immediate threat to the stability of the system, but in the long-run the buildup of centrifugal ethnic forces may well contribute to a major change in the nature of the Soviet state as it is today, and may even lead to its eventual disintegration. At present, the ethnicity-generated change is slow and evolutionary, even as the forces pressing for it are accelerating. There has been a degree of grudging and conditional recognition for ethnic demands in Moscow but no real accommodations, largely, one suspects, because the leadership cannot find adequate solution to the problem and any changes in the present system may open the floodgates of nationalism. Should there be a violent change in the status quo, however, ethnicity may well trigger a revolutionary change.

The subject is too complex to be explored fully in a short article. Here an attempt is made to discuss the dimensions and the nature of the ethnic conflict in the Soviet Union, with special emphasis on its sources of growth and the dynamics of ethnic interaction as they evolve under the "rules of the game" imposed by the system.

Salient Variables

Background

The colonial heritage of imperial Russia continues to affect relations between the Russians and non-Russians in the Soviet Union even today. The Russian colonial expansion extended into areas geographically contiguous, but followed a familiar pattern of pursuit of economic and political interests followed by conquest. Most of the non-Russian border areas attempted to break away after the 1917 revolution but were reconquered by the new Bolshevik government in the name of "proletarian unity." Those that did gain independence, such as the three Baltic states, were reincorporated in World War II, at which time also the Soviet boundaries were extended westward to include the Western Ukraine and Belorussia and Moldavia. Despite an effort, in the Soviet period, at an across-the-board modernization and equalization, aspects of colonial relationships survive, inclusive of attitudes. The multiethnic mosaic of Soviet population today is the result of past colonial conquest, the historical—frequently the living—memory of which is a part of the ethnic consciousness of the non-Russian peoples.[3]

The last (1970) Soviet census listed more than 100 nations and nationalities. The Russians constituted 53 percent of the total population (a decline of 1 percent since the previous census of 1959), but 21 other national groups numbered more than 1 million people each (see Table 1). Of these, the Ukrainians (40.8 million), the Uzbeks (9.2 million), and the Belorussians (9.1 million) were the most numerous; in the overall

ETHNICITY IN THE SOVIET UNION

TABLE 1

USSR. MAJOR ETHNIC GROUPS, 1970: NUMBERS, URBANIZATION, SETTLEMENT
PATTERN AND COEFFICIENTS OF DEVELOPMENT

ETHNIC GROUP	NUMBERS		URBANIZATION IN % OF POPULATION		SETTLEMENT DISTRIBUTION IN % OF GROUP MEMBERS RESIDENT IN OWN NATIONAL UNIT*	COEFFICIENT OF DEVELOPMENT BY REPUBLIC IN 1965
	ABS. FIGURES (MILLIONS)	% OF THE TOTAL	BY THE GROUP	BY RE- PUBLIC		
Russians (1)	129.0	53.3	68	64	83	1.05
Ukrainians (1)	40.8	16.9	49	56	86	1.04
Uzbeks (4)	9.2	3.8	25	37	84	.71
Belorussians (1)	9.1	3.7	44	46	80	1.01
Tatars	5.9	2.4	55	n.a.	26	n.a.
Kazakhs (4)	5.3	2.2	27	52	80	.88
Azerbaijani (2)	4.4	1.8	40	51	86	.71
Armenians (2)	3.6	1.5	65	61	60	.84
Georgians (2)	3.2	1.2	44	48	97	.87
Moldavians	2.7	1.1	20	33	85	.97
Lithuanians (3)	2.7	1.1	47	53	94	1.02
Jews	2.2	0.9	98	n.a.	no unit	n.a.
Tadzhiks (4)	2.1	0.9	26	38	76	.69
Germans	1.8	0.8	46	n.a.	no unit	n.a.
Turkmen (4)	1.5	0.6	31	48	93	.77
Kirgiz (4)	1.5	0.6	15	38	89	.76
Latvians (3)	1.4	0.6	53	64	94	1.17
Poles (1)	1.2	0.5	45	n.a.	no unit	n.a.
Estonians (3)	1.0	0.4	55	66	92	1.14

SOURCE: Columns 2–6 based on *Results of the 1970 All-Union Census*, vol. 4 (Moscow: Statistika, 1973). Column 7 adapted from K. Vermishev, "On the Level of Economic Development of the Union Republics," *Voprosy Ekonomiki*, no. 4 (Moscow), 1970, p. 128. The coefficient was calculated by the Soviet scholar as the ratio of the republic's share of total USSR gross domestic product in 1965 to the share of the given republic's population in total Soviet population in the same year.

NOTE: The USSR population total was 241.7 million; urbanization—56 percent of the population. The national groups which have union republics are in italics. The Russian republic is known as the Russian Soviet Federated Socialist Republic (RSFSR), because it contains most of the lower type national units, inclusive of Tatar ASSR. Three more groups number over one million people: the Chuvashi (1.7), the Mordvinians (1.3), and the Bashkirs (1.3). All have autonomous republics within RSFSR. Key: (1) Slavs; (2) Caucasians; (3) Baltics; (4) Central Asians.

* Except for the Slavs, the major part of union republics' national groups nonresident in their republic are settled in the neighboring areas.

mix the Slavs had an overwhelming majority of 74 percent. Under the 1936 USSR constitution,[4] the ethnic groups of any significant size have had their own national administrative-territorial units: there are 15 union republics (SSR) (see Table 1), 20 autonomous republics (ASSR), 8 autonomous provinces (AO), and 10 national regions. Not all of the major nations, however, have an appropriate national unit, either because of geographic dispersal (the Jews and the Poles) or for political reasons (the Germans and the Crimean Tatars).[5]

The officially sponsored policy of inter-republic migration and ethnic intermixture has affected the basic national settlement pattern of major groups remarkably little in the sixty years of Soviet power. A preponderant majority of most ethnic groups still live in their national areas or in the regions immediately contiguous (see Table 1). The Russians are the most significant exception, and the eastward shift of the Soviet population since 1917 occurred largely because of the geographic mobility of the Russian group, who now dominate the urban and industrial centers throughout the country. A number of Ukrainians and Belorussians also migrated eastward; among other groups only the Armenians have shown a certain geographic mobility. The Jews, who are almost totally urbanized (see Table 1), are a special case.

Levels of ethnic consciousness and economic and social development vary significantly among major Soviet ethnic groups as do the patterns of their national cultures. Along with the historical nations that had enjoyed periods of independent statehood, such as the three Baltic republics, Armenia, and Georgia, the Soviet peoples include the Western Slavs and Moldavians, historically subject to the contending influences, respectively, of Russia and Poland, Russia and the Ottoman Empire (later Romania); the Turkic and Iranian groups of Central Asia, the ancient culture of which was destroyed by the thirteenth-century Mongol invasion and who now are developing separate national identities. The dominant Soviet culture is rooted in the Russian Byzantine heritage, but the non-Russians have retained strong traditional cultural identities of their own. These range from the Scandinavian culture and Lutheranism of Estonia and Latvia and Catholicism of Lithuania, to ancient indigenous traditions and Orthodox Christianity of Georgia and Armenia, Western Orthodoxy of the Ukraine, Belorussia, and Moldavia, and Islam of Central Asia and Azerbaijan.

Policy Impact and Ethnicity

The growth of the ethnic self-assertion of major Soviet national groups that became visible in the sixties and seventies is as much an unexpected by-product of Soviet policies—reinforced by examples of ethnic self-assertion throughout the world—as it is the outcome of traditional ethnic hostilities. Paradoxically, instead of the expected "internationalization," many of the Soviet policies aiming at the transformation of society and the building of socialism have served to stimulate ethnic polarization. Five key policy decisions have had a direct impact on the growth of national self-assertion in the multiethnic Soviet society: the legitimization of the system in class-based international ideology of Marxism-Leninism; the federal state–unitary party dichotomy; the policy of accelerated modernization and economic development; the cultural policy aimed at the development of "national forms" of all the Soviet ethnic groups; and the dynamic post–World War II expansionist foreign policy.

Marxist-Leninist ideology postulates unity based on a common working-class identity (proletarian internationalism), which overrides particular national political loyalties. The latter are expected to disappear once socialism is established, but the process, which involves a change in attitudes, cannot be achieved overnight. Thus, in the meantime, while the ethnic-based sense of political identity is seen as a vestigial, transitory, and gradually disappearing phenomenon, its continuous existence is legitimate and cannot be denied. The dynamics of relations between the traditional national loyalties and the new Soviet one are seen to be developing on a "rapprochement-merger" dialectical continuum. This means a process of all the Soviet nations and nationalities "ever growing closer together" (rapprochement) that is achieved through the "flowering" of their own national socialist cultures, the reciprocal "enrichment" of which serves to develop a common base, all of which is supposed to lead to an eventual merger into a one common Soviet identity. The ideological image of class-based integration, however, precludes a return to the Russian national ethos as the basis of Soviet political loyalty. The de facto Russian content of Soviet norms, value systems, and patterns of behavior cannot be legitimately acknowledged, even though a claim is always made that the Russians, as the most "progressive," are the leading nation in the Soviet family of nations. The claim partially offsets the ideological handicap, but it also serves to increase non-Russians' resentment of the Russian hegemony.

Vladimir Ilyich Lenin's compromise formula of a federal state run by a unitary party (a resolution of an endless debate within the party in the early twenties between assimilationists and the autonomists) has built the country's administrative structure on an ethnic base. A brilliant solution to a seemingly insoluble national problem at the time, in the long run it provided a territorial and economic base for the growth of the ethnic demands and political structures for national interests' aggregation and their articulation at the federal level. The federal administration is Russian-dominated, and in pursuit of their local interests the republican authorities tend to identify with their national constituency. The old ethnic conflict has been reinforced by the new administrative one, especially because in the post-Stalin period the ethnic coloration of the republics' state and party apparatus became increasingly local, although the outsiders (mostly ethnic Russians) continue to occupy strategic power positions there.[6] The conflict is evident not only in the state administration but also within the theoretically unitary party apparatus.

The modernization policy has transformed and developed the Soviet economy and restructured the society through industrialization, collectivization, urbanization, and the development of mass education and communications systems and social services, affecting all of the Soviet peoples. All the major ethnic groups now are better off economically, have access to educational and social benefits, and have evolved modern elites that participate in the power structure. But, given differentials in the take-off point, the rates of social mobilization have been uneven, and the relative comparative standing within the country of ethnic groups has not changed. Economic and social development indicators still stand the highest in the Baltic northwest and the European republics in general and the lowest in Central Asian southeast[7] (see Table 1). The growing perception, by the new ethnic elites, of their relative deprivation and of their second-class political status vis-à-vis the Russians feeds ethnic antagonisms, while improved standards and growing access to means of social and self-fulfillment by the masses stimulate the familiar rising expectations. Increasingly, the ethnic base is being perceived as the instrument for the gratification of the new ambitions by the elites as well as their ethnic constituency, forging a new bond between them, and giving a new meaning to the traditional sense of ethnic identity and national loyalties.

Modernization also has had differential impact on the dynamics of demographic change. The Russians, and other more developed national groups, have shown a decline (in the last intercensal period, 1959-70) in natural growth rates, while the high fertility rates of the least developed groups, in Central Asia primarily, but also in the Caucasus, are among the highest in the world, the result of cultural (Islam) as much as of social development factors. The shift in the demographic pattern has already had political and economic implications. The Russians' weight in the population at large and in the population of the eastern and southern republics has declined. The depopulation of rural areas of European Russia is reaching crisis proportions, and the shortage of labor, particularly skilled labor, is felt in the more developed republics and in the Eastern Siberia–Far Eastern region of the RSFSR, where the Soviet economic and strategic buildup has focused in the seventies. At the same time a major pool of unskilled rural-based manpower is building up in Central Asia. Attempts at a resolution of impending manpower crisis may have far-reaching political effects. Cultural factors militate against a natural flow of economic migration (the

Muslims of Central Asia do not want to leave their area), while
overall political, economic, and strategic considerations
make a massive long-range investment to build up manufacturing industries utilizing local manpower in the southeastern
regions unlikely.

In the implementation of the national form–socialist content dualism, the Soviet cultural policy aimed at developing the
national cultures of the major ethnic groups, which would
become vehicles for the dissemination of socialist culture
common to all. National languages were developed and
modernized, and a system of mass education was provided in
local languages. In some cases this involved the formation of
virtually new languages on the basis of regional dialects—as in
the case of the Turkic peoples of Central Asia—and written and
oral culture forms and fine arts, based on traditional patterns,
were revived or developed. The overall thrust of ideological
socialization, however, was marked, for all practical purposes
by cultural Russification. The study of the Russian language,
the common Soviet language and the "language of civiliza-
tion," has been promoted vigorously; linguistic modernization
of national languages took the road of incorporation of
Russian-derived vocabulary and grammatical forms and
introduction of the Cyrillic alphabet, except in the case of
established historical languages; Russian cultural forms have
been held as models to be emulated by other groups.

The policy has been extremely successful, but not in a way
desired or expected by its initiators. A virtual renaissance of
national cultures took place among all the major non-Russian
national groups, a renaissance which has become an integral
part of their new national self-assertion and a vehicle for the
expression of their newly formed national pride. Bilingualism
spread for functional reasons but not the eventually expected
linguistic assimilation into the Russian language. Paradoxically, it was the cultural content rather than form that has been
affected by the new ethnic cultural renaissance, resulting in the
development of officially approved common Soviet forms, the

content of which has been increasingly determined by each group's traditional ethnic heritage.

After World War II the dynamics of Soviet foreign policy combined a drive for an extension of political influence of the USSP as a great power with an appeal to internationalism of the working class and all progressive forces abroad. The East European socialist states (established in the wake of Soviet armed invasion in 1945) are members of the Socialist Commonwealth, led by the USSR. Within the world Communist movement, Soviet policy has attempted to reestablish its previously undisputed leadership, lost in the aftermath of the death of J.V. Stalin and the challenge by the Chinese. At the same time, the Soviet Union has come to play an increasingly important role in the Third World as a leader of all "peace loving" and "anti-imperialist" forces. There are contradictions, however, between an internationalist foreign policy and domestic national integration, which have contributed to the growth of ethnic self-assertion within the Soviet Union as minority groups became aware of examples of successful national self-assertion within the Communist movement and in the Third World.

Theoretically, relations of the states within the Communist bloc and the Communist international movement in general have been governed by the same principle of proletarian internationalism that applies in domestic national relations. In this context the relative sovereignty enjoyed by the East Europeans provides a tempting example to Soviet ethnic groups and a model to strive for in their search for greater national autonomy within the system. The temptation has been enhanced in the seventies by Soviet efforts at greater integration of the bloc, with its emphasis on the identical nature of "fraternal ties" on both sides of the border[8] as well as a start of direct exchanges between the republics and East European states. In relations with the nonruling parties, particularly since the birth of Eurocommunism, the Soviet Union has had to make concessions to polycentrism, including recognition of other parties' right to their own "road to socialism." Ideological concessions lend legitimacy to the republics' quest for greater autonomy, and East European nationalism tends to be contagious.

Finally, in relations with Third World countries, the avowed Soviet support for national self-determination has not passed unnoticed at home, especially because the republics, particularly the Asian ones, are an important asset in foreign policy as models of Soviet-type development as well as justification for the claim that the Soviet Union is an Asian as well as European power. The impact of Third World contacts is particularly important because of numerous exchanges between them and the republics. Members of non-Russian minorities, who feature prominently in Soviet foreign delegations, can thus gain a firsthand knowledge of conditions abroad and can compare their own viability as independent entities (in terms of economic base, infrastructure, educated elites, and so on) with newly independent Third World countries.

Ethnic Conflict and the "Rules of the Game"

Dimensions

In party and state relations in the USSR, ethnicity has become the main base for interest group demands, a phenomenon familiar to the students of ethnic relations worldwide.[9] In the absence of institutionalized channels for interest articulation, the republics are the focus for the aggregation of local interests in all spheres of social life; when articulated by local spokesmen, these invariably acquire ethnic overtones. The spokesmen are the new ethnic elites. Fully "socialized" for functional purposes, including fluency in the Russian language and ideological medium, these elites are members of the establishment in their republics—some even move up to the federal level—but invariably their position and power is circumscribed by the presence of the ubiquitous Russians. It is the Russian "fact," probably more than any other single factor, that has been the catalyst in the ethnic self-assertion of the national elites, especially because Russian nationalism also has been on the rise. Since they are partners in the system, the thrust of it is not directed at the systemic status quo but only at the constraints imposed within by Russian hegemony. The aim of ethnic self-assertion of the elites is the maximization of autonomy that is formally theirs constitutionally and the realization of the self-determination principle enshrined in the ideology; if an idea of separatism enters the equation, it is not openly articulated. Ethnic demands are uttered in the systemic double talk familiar to all and concern matters that affect local interests. In a system as highly centralized as that of the Soviet Union, a greater share in decision making at the federal level is of great concern, as is a devolution of power from the federal to the republican level, formally or through personal "pull" upstairs.

The elites' relationship with the Russians is ambiguous; the majority now in the republics' authorities, they resent controls imposed by outsiders and attempt to bypass and counteract them—frequently with considerable success. At the same time, the relationship is close, and collaboration in defense of local interests, as seen from an administrator's viewpoint, is not uncommon. Those who made it in the federal service may serve as spokesmen for ethnic interests in Moscow if representing their own republic; otherwise, they tend to merge into the prevalent Russian coloration. Those serving in other national areas frequently champion federal interests more assiduously than do the ethnic Russians.

The elites' ties with their national constituency are also ambiguous. There is a sense of common interests that seems to be growing vis-à-vis the "they" in Moscow and cultural ties which, by all accounts, appear to be stronger than in comparable situations elsewhere. In the Central Asian republics, for example, there is evidence that most members of local elites have emerged directly from a rural background. At the same time, however, in their daily work the elites act as agents of the central authorities enforcing policies which make them unpopular with the populace.

In the past there was relatively little contact between the various ethnic elites, except within the federal administration. This has been changing, however, under the impact of the rapprochement policy adopted since 1961. Contacts are now frequent, especially on a regional basis, but there is no evidence of an incipient common front, except in the case of Central Asian Muslims. Foreign contacts, as pointed out above, are also more frequent. Those with Eastern Europe and the developing countries have been important for the diffusion of new ideas and undoubtedly exposed Soviet ethnic elites to the virus of nationalism.

Legitimization

Ethnic self-assertion in the Soviet Union seeks legitimacy in two sources: the constitutional-legal framework and ideological principles. The USSR constitution gives the republics the right to conduct their own foreign relations and to have their own military establishments; the first was never genuinely exercised; the latter was precluded de facto by the 1938 military reform.[10] It also gives the formal right to secede, which has had no value in reality. The enumerated federal powers are all-embracing, leaving little residuary authority to republics. Even so, there are numerous minor provisions formally involving the republics—such as republican legislative bodies' approval of federal decrees or of local boundary changes. The genuine exercise of these provisions is one of the targets of the elites. The subject of secession has not been raised formally, but two Kirgiz scholars have discussed their republic's right to do so in legal terms.

The focus of the demands for self-assertion is in the ideological sphere. The revival of Leninism as the ruling myth has provided an opening for the ethnic spokesmen to resurrect Lenin's views on the national self-determination principle and on national equality under the federal formula. Numerous treatises have appeared in impeccable ideological terms, some explicit in their resentment of Russian hegemony.[11] There is also much discussion of old Leninist policy of autonomization of political cadres (*Korenizatsia*), abandoned under Stalin, as an example to be emulated. The current policy of rapprochement is also used by ethnic spokesmen in support of their demands by way of emphasizing the "flowering" part of the formula, which presupposes full development of particular ethnic cultures. The current line vis-à-vis Eastern Europe and the CPSU dispute with Eurocommunism are watched carefully for changes of wording in current slogans which may provide an opening in the battle for greater autonomy. In general, ethnic spokesmen are at pains to differentiate between their own brand of socialist ethnicity, which is "progressive," and the capitalist one (bourgeois nationalism), which is vigorously condemned. This does not necessarily protect them from being eventually criticized by federal authorities as bourgeois nationalists or from being purged.

Political Dynamics

In the political arena, ethnic demands center less on the exercise of formal constitutional powers—although these are desirable—and more on the exercise of the real power within the party structure, focusing particularly on access to decision making and on control of cadres (personnel) policy. In this quest ethnic leaders increasingly court the support of their ethnic constituency; this is sought among local bureaucracies, but also among the populace, particularly on issues related to national culture. Pressures for greater share in decision making are centered in the republics but extend also to the federal arena. This shows in more open articulation of economic and cultural demands. Control of appointments—traditionally a preserve of the party[12] with selections made at a level higher than the appointments—is a political and highly sensitive matter. Here demands for greater autonomization and a reduction of outsiders in politically important positions are stated obliquely, a battle punctuated by recurrent purges of too outspoken or too ambitious ethnic leaders.

The extent of political change brought about by ethnic pressures may be observed by comparing the current with the pre-1956 situation, even though qualitatively they are small and far below the level of real political autonomy. Outsiders are still, inevitably, occupying the key position of Central Committee second secretary (control of cadres) in all republics, but their ratio has declined in other key positions in party and state hierarchies. In the meantime ethnic elite members within have been vigorously promoting local cadres for positions throughout the republics, squeezing out the Russians. Complaints about the latter practice appear sporadically in the press. At the federal level the republics' first secretaries, invariably of local ethnic origin, are all members of the CPSU Central Committee (the usage that dates back to Stalin's period), but those representing the key republics or regions are also member or candidate members of the ruling Politburo. The Ukraine contingent has been particularly strong there, because both N. S. Khrushchev and L. I. Brezhnev rose to power from their local base in the Ukraine. In 1976 Central Asia was represented by the Uzbek and Kazakh party first secretaries; Belorussian and Azerbaijani first secretaries were also included. On the state side, heads of the republican state and judicial hierarchies have been ex-officio members of equivalent federal bodies since the sixties. But, although the republican state and party representation at the federal level has improved, they are still a minority in the ruling state and party bodies. Support by the hierarchies of major republics is a significant factor in factional struggles at the top; it diminishes as one of the Politburo leaders is able to achieve a degree of personal ascendancy. The Byzantine character of Soviet politics emphasizes the importance of personal pull and factional membership for republican leaders: each new "boss" appoints his men, and the success of this or that republic in having its demands met frequently depends on the quality of its leaderships' contacts at the top. Georgia, for example, has traditionally enjoyed a higher degree of autonomy because the late Joseph Stalin was a Georgian; its degree of autonomy has survived relatively untouched, despite successive purges of ethnic first secretaries there.

Economic Demands

In economic relations the ethnic conflict centers on disputes concerning resource allocation and distribution. Almost every republic would like to maximize its share of investment and to minimize the share of its products allocated to other regions. with total disregard (if one is to believe Soviet sources) of the general interest. The issue is particularly aggravated in the case of the economically strongest non-Russian republic, the Ukraine, the leaders of which resent the transfer of its resources to other regions.[13] It is also crucial in the case of the least developed southeastern republics, laboring under a handicap of being primarily a resource base for the manufacturing industries of European Russia. They agitate for major long-range capital investment and equalization. Because of the recent population explosion there, they argue now from stronger positions but, so far, unsuccessfully. In general there is evidence of central planners being tired of ethnic-based parochial demands, and arguments appear in economic journals that republics are obsolete for purposes of efficient economic management. Their economic role was left unchallenged, however, in the 1973 reform of economic management, despite streamlining, and no basic changes have appeared in the June 1977 draft of the new constitution. Because of sporadic evidence of heated disputes on the subject, the absence of change indicates the weight of the republics' vested interests in the system. The economic battle also centers around annual and quinquennial plan fulfillment indicators, with habitual doctoring of statistical results in their favor not only by enterprises and federally run industries, but also by republics.

Social Relations

The pattern of compact ethnic settlement and the concentration of ethnic population in rural areas has favored the survival of traditional agents of socialization, and there is evidence of a high level of social alienation between the local and immigrant communities in the national areas, which spills over into urban settings despite considerable ethnic intermixture there. Traditional social patterns, values, and modes of behavior are also reinforced by the survival of religion and its close identification with the sense of ethnic identity of most major ethnic groups. Evidence of alienation is seen in patterns of social intercourse between the local and immigrant communities and the low incidence of intermarriage, particularly between the Slavic and Asian groups. Among some groups social behavior has become an ethnic weapon, as in the case of Central Asian Muslims, whose high fertility rates, conditioned by their relatively low level of modernization, persist also in the urban setting for cultural and political reasons.

At the same time, however, the impact of socioeconomic advancement has greatly increased social mobility of ethnic groups, causing rural exodus to the cities. This, coupled with cultural alienation, has served to intensify ethnic conflict in social relations in an urban setting where the Russians have been a dominant element. Increasingly, there is competition for jobs not only in the political arena but also in economic-technical and professional spheres—heretofore the domain of the Russians in all but the two northern Baltic republics and, in part, Georgia and Armenia, because of their superior qualifications, but reinforced in all of the republics by political preference in filling sensitive and important positions. Because of the autonomization of republican power structures, political preference now works both ways, in favor of local candidates as much as immigrants, depending on who controls the hiring and at what level—a tug of war which is another source of growing ethnic conflict.

Cultural Arena

The evidence of ethnic self-assertion is the most open and

intense in the cultural sphere. Cultural conflict is in many ways a substitute for an open political conflict, the appearance of which is muted for systemic reasons. As noted above, all of the republics have had a cultural renaissance (it has been least pronounced in Belorussia and Moldavia). Adherence to national languages exceeds 90 percent among all of the major union republic nations, with the exception of Ukrainians and Belorussians,among whom it is in the 80 percent plus bracket, indicating the degree of emigration from their national areas. In republics where the Russification of ethnic languages has gone the furthest—in the Ukraine and in Central Asia—there is a vigorous language "purification" campaign aimed at substitution of national terms for Russian-derived words and grammatical usages. Local language primary education continues to develop along with Russian-language schools, and there are increasing demands for the introduction of local language instructors in technical and professional secondary and higher educational establishments, where it is now conducted primarily in the Russian language. Numbers and circulation of local language newspapers and periodicals and monographs have been increasing, with some republics acting as regional pacesetters. In the literature and fine arts, there has been a revival of traditional themes, symbolism, and imagery and a marked absence of themes dealing with the current socialist reality and internationalism, as documented by official criticism. In historiography a battle is raging between the binding official line that consigns most traditional heroes and events (especally those that testify to past resistance to Russian encroachments) to a reactionary category and local historians' attempt at a more objective interpretation based on research in local archives. Dispute over the interpretation of national history has been most pronounced in the Ukraine, the Caucasian republics, and Central Asia. The significant aspect of the ethnic conflict as revealed in the cultural sphere has been an apparent support for cultural self-assertion by the republican party authorities, the approval of which is necessary for anything that appears in print or in any public form. Official criticism, when it comes, is usually generated in Moscow and appears a considerable time after the event in question has taken place.[14]

Trends and Prospects

It is clear that under the impact of ongoing change the dual "national in form, socialist in content" framework of the Soviet state has been gradually losing its functionality in the area it was meant to resolve, namely, that of ethnic relations. Instead of an expected unionwide integration, it has stimulated the forces of ethnicity, the containment of which is proving increasingly difficult. The process has advanced at differential rates among the several major ethnic groups: currently it is most pronounced in the Ukraine and in the Baltic republics, with Georgia and Armenia not far behind, but there are signs that in a relatively short time Central Asia may well move into the forefront of ethnic turmoil. Many aspects of ethnic self-assertion in the Soviet Union are directly comparable to those in other multiethnic areas, and its eventual outcome may be the same as in other societies, where the conflict has been more open and further advanced.

The policy dilemma for the Soviet leadership is evident from its almost complete immobility on the issue, as seen in the pursuance of past policies, punctuated by halfhearted re-pressions. Soviet leaders find themselves in a position when even small concessions may open the floodgates of a major change, and continue therefore to maintain a hope that eventually the ideologically predicted integration will take place after all—a hope that, in view of similar experience elsewhere, appears illusory. Forces for ethnic change now push for the evolution of the system. Should this be denied, however, as seems likely in the face of the current leadership's resistance to it, the resulting pressures may eventually lead to an explosion. Latent separatism may also come to the fore in case of a major international upheaval.

Notes

1. See Vernon V. Aspaturian, *Process and Power in Soviet Foreign Policy* (Boston: Little, Brown and Co., 1971), chs. 14 and 19.

2. Mikhail Suslov, "The Social Sciences—A Combat Arm of the Party in the Building of Communism," *Kommunist* (Moscow), January 1972, pp. 18-30.

3. In the twenties Soviet historiography recognized and condemned past Russian imperialism. The interpretation changed in the thirties. Now the conquest is presented as an objectively "good" and historically "progressive" phenomenon, because it involved the minorities in the Russian Revolution, thus enabling them to become a part of the world's first socialist state.

4. The draft of the new constitution, made public June 4, 1977, did not introduce any changes in the federal structure.

5. The Crimean Tatars (deported along with the Volga Germans during World War II for alleged collaboration with the invaders) are a subgroup of a Tatar national group. There is a Tatar ASSR for the main Tatar group, the Volga Tatars. Both the deported groups were rehabilitated in the sixties but remain in exile, and their autonomous republics were not restored.

6. In the forties and fifties there was a pattern in personnel placement in national republics: top positions in party and government bodies were reserved for local nationals; the second-in-command positions, for federal representatives, mostly Russians. See Seweryn Bialer, "How Russians Rule Russia," *Problems of Communism* (September-October 1964), pp. 45-52; Yaroslav Bilinsky, "The Rulers and the Ruled," ibid. (September-October 1967), pp. 16-26; and this author's *Russia and Nationalism in Central Asia: The Case of Tadzhikistan* (Baltimore, Md.: The Johns Hopkins University Press, 1970), ch. 4.

7. See Zev Katz, Rosemarie Rogers, Frederic Harned, eds., *Handbook of Major Soviet Nationalities* (New York: The Free Press, 1975), appendix, pp. 452-58, and 462-64.

8. See this author's "Socialist Internationalism in Eastern Europe—A New Stage," *Survey*, vol. 98, no. 1 (Winter 1976), pp. 38-54.

9. See Nathan Glazer and Daniel P. Moynihan, *Ethnicity: Theory and Experience* (Cambridge, Mass.: Harvard University Press, 1975), p. 7.

10. Prior to 1938 some units were formed on an ethnic basis, but the reform instituted ethnically mixed, Russian-language units. Some ethnic units were formed during World War II on an ad hoc basis.

11. Of the latter, the best known in the West is a monograph by a Ukrainian journalist, Ivan Dzyuba, *Internationalism or Russification?* (London: Weidenfeld and Nicolson, 1968), written for and circulated in the Ukrainian party organization, which was later published in the West. Dzyuba has been imprisoned and has since recanted.

12. The party's control of appointments, the so-called *nomenklatura*, extends not only to political jobs but also to all important positions in the economy and in society in general.

13. Petro Shelest, the Ukrainian party first secretary, who was purged in 1972, was accused of economic as well as cultural nationalism. His additional problem was that he belonged to a "wrong" Ukrainian faction.

14. Considerable literature exists in the English language on Soviet ethnicity and on ethnic conflict in the Soviet Union. For most comprehensive recent coverage, see Katz, Rogers, Harned, *Handbook of Major Soviet Nationalities;* and George W. Simmonds, ed., *Nationalism in the USSR and Eastern Europe in the Era of Brezhnev and Kosygin* (Detroit, Mich.: The University of Detroit Press, 1977).

Index